Van der Graaf Generator

# Pawn Hearts

## The full story of the 1971 classic

Paolo Carnelli

sonicbondpublishing.com

Sonicbond Publishing Limited
www.sonicbondpublishing.co.uk
Email: info@sonicbondpublishing.co.uk

First Italian edition: December 2013

First English edition: December 2019


This edition 2025
First Published in the United States 2025

British Library Cataloguing in Publication Data:
A Catalogue record for this book is available from the British Library



ISBN 978-1-78952-357-7



Typeset in ITC Garamond Std & ITC Avant Garde Gothic
Printed and bound in England

Graphic design and typesetting: Full Moon Media



**Follow us on social media:**
Twitter: https://twitter.com/SonicbondP
Instagram: www.instagram.com/sonicbondpublishing_/
Facebook: www.facebook.com/SonicbondPublishing/

Linktree QR code:

## Acknowledgements

English translation by Simone Morelli & Paolo Carnelli.
English text revision by Sean Kelly.
Thanks to Antonio De Sarno, Maria Grazia Umbro,
Alessandra Bersiani, Francesco Pepe.

Alice told Peter that a letter had arrived that morning.
It was from a young lad in Manchester who had left home because
his parents would not let him play *Pawn Hearts* in the house.
***Melody Maker*, 7 April 1973**

# Foreword

*Pawn Hearts* is simply the summation of the best tendencies, musical and philosophical, of the early Van der Graaf Generator, the album where it all crystallised for them on three epic tracks, 'Lemmings', 'Man-Erg' and the album side-long opus 'A Plague Of Lighthouse Keepers', which pre-dated Genesis' side long 'Supper's Ready' by at least a year.

This album has come to define the best progressive rock, and as such, is essential listening for anyone attempting to come to grips with the genre. 'Lighthouse Keepers' is, for me, the *creme de la creme* in arrangement and execution, Peter's compelling vocals limning the lonely introspection of the lighthouse keeper, superbly reinforced by keyboards, woodwinds and drums. Passages crisscross and shock in a stentorian manner as deranged alternates with murmuring languorous meditative drift, with the over-arching contour of the track touching the far shores of heaven and hell. Peter's heartfelt and bizarre vocals on the album are clearly an influence on the first generation of UK punk belters, including Mark Smith, Johnny Rotten and Howard Devoto.

A nearly flawless masterpiece.

Gary Lucas

# Van der Graaf Generator
# Pawn Hearts

**Contents**

# Introduction

It was the beginning of 2007 and the Peter Hammill & Van der Graaf Generator Study Group, founded by Marina and Emilio Maestri five years before, was still going ahead full steam. After the extraordinary – and expensive – concert by Nic Potter and David Jackson that took place in the summer of 2006 in Guastalla (Italy), we met to decide what the next goal was going to be. We realised, and surprisingly, too, that although the Study Group had been able to organise quite a good amount of live events during its existence, the 'research' moments were still missing. We started to think about how we could fill this gap. Luckily, fate was on our side: just in the same period, Mr. Ricardo Odriozola, a lecturer from the Grieg Academy in Bergen (Norway), published a detailed essay on the Van der Graaf Generator album *Pawn Hearts*, also providing sheet music for every track that was included on the original record. Although a *Pawn Hearts* anniversary was not planned in 2007 – the album was released exactly 36 years before in October 1971 – we decided to devote a full weekend in Guastalla to meetings, lectures and in-depth analyses of the album.

The result was amazing: the *Dark Figures Running* lyrics book, released by the Study Group in 2005, had already proved how much was still to be discovered lyrically on *Pawn Hearts*, but during the two-day event at Teatro Ruggeri in Guastalla, so many new topics arose that even the hardest Van der Graaf Generator fan returned home having learned something new. The event featured a reading of the *Pawn Hearts* lyrics and many specific lectures focused on different aspects of the album, such as the meaning of the lyrics, the artwork and the music. There was also a real exhibit showcasing selected memorabilia from the early 1970s. It was then, during the *Pawn Hearts* weekend, that I realised for the first time how much the album was able to tell us about the incredible talent of those four very young musicians in their early 20s, living their lives in the challenging and frenetic music world of the early 1970s. They were signed to a young record label that perhaps kept them a bit short on money but which was, at the same time, more than happy to let them follow their own artistic path.

*The Least We Can Do Is Wave To Each Other*, the second Van der Graaf Generator album released by Charisma Records in 1969, and *Pawn Hearts* were released only two years apart, but much had changed in such a short period. Hammill's writing withdrew from those pastoral interludes ('Out Of My Book') and those romantic and heartfelt drifts ('Refugees') that Charisma boss Tony Stratton Smith was so fond of. Hammill was aiming to go beyond the typical pop song structure, writing songs with a flow in which sections are not repeated (*Melody Maker,* 8/1972 – 'Van breaks down: a Peter Hammill interview by Richard Williams'). It's no coincidence that, just a couple of months before *Pawn Hearts* was released, Hammill decided to put down every single 'song' he had not recorded yet with the band. The result – his first solo album, *Fool's Mate* – was released in July 1971. The aim was clear: to close an artistic chapter and start focusing on a new direction to follow from then onward.

What Van der Graaf Generator gave birth to during their stay in the 'haunted house' in Crowborough in the summer of 1971 was amazing, especially with regard to a track like 'A Plague Of Lighthouse Keepers'. That's why, in retrospect, I think that it is correct to see *Pawn Hearts* more as a leap into the unknown instead of a gradual and pondered landing. It was a radical turning point mastered by pure instinct that was absolutely against every kind of commercial reasoning.

The fact that *Pawn Hearts*, after getting poor reviews in the UK, made it to the Italian top ten (the number-one position that is still often attributed to the album was indeed achieved only on the charts compiled by the Italian magazine *Ciao 2001*, based on a selected number of record shops) and that the band played several sold out shows in Italy is just another part of this incredible and unpredictable story, a tale that I wrote about in my previous book *Van der Graaf Generator – La Biografia Italiana* (published by Arcana in January 2013). To be honest, the book was meant to also include a whole chapter dedicated to the *Pawn Hearts* album as, after the Guastalla weekend, I was able to collect further information on the album for a lecture I gave at Casa del Jazz in Rome in September 2012. Working on the seminar, I realised that a single chapter was not going to be enough to document all the sparks flowing from that masterpiece. So, the idea of a full essay arose, which would aim to dig all around the album, piece after piece, part after part – the story, the music, the artwork, the lyrics – trying to shed some light on the characters that took part in the making of it: the above-mentioned Charisma Boss Tony Stratton Smith, the brilliant producer John Anthony, the irreverent and creative painter Paul Whitehead, the impassive guitar master Robert Fripp, the 'fifth Beatle' Sir George Martin. They were all precious pawns in that particular chess game that, as the Italian editor Vittore Baroni wrote in a nice retrospective article back in the 1980s, Peter Hammill still goes on mastering today.

## A Historical Setting

Let's rewind the tape. Let's place the needle on the vinyl and play the first track from an album hosted in colourful and imaginative packaging, with a sleeve packed with small figures floating into space. The sound comes from the distance: in an unusual way, the arpeggio provided by the acoustic guitar rises slowly from the dark on the left. A chanting sax on the right seems to call us to follow its path. After 20 seconds, here comes a voice in the wind that talks to us, depicting an apocalyptic vision...

### October 1971

It was just a couple of years before that the new UK music scene gave birth to the forerunners of a change that would be contagious and extreme in equal measure. The Beatles' 1967 album *Sgt. Pepper* paved the way: the three-minute standard song, conceived for the mighty 7" record, was crushed by a completely different attitude, one which aimed to expand musical ideas and break free from the rigid radio format. Twelve-inch vinyl, able to contain over 45 minutes of music, became the media that this new generation of musicians paid more attention to. As every vinyl side can last up to 25 minutes, the time boundary for a newly shaped kind of 'song' had been greatly extended: the 'suite', a giant canvas ready to be flooded by a kaleidoscope of sounds and colours.

After the experiment with *Ummagumma* (1969), for example, Pink Floyd wanted to search for a new and original way to express their art. The four musicians got in touch with Ron Geesin, an avant-garde composer from Scotland, and at the end of 1969, they started working on a new piece of music called 'The Amazing Pudding'. The new composition was played live at Croydon Town Hall in London on 18 January and some days after, on 23 January, at the Theatre Des Champe Elysèes in Paris. At that point, the band decided to morph it into a full suite, also with the help of an orchestra and a choir. Geesin was involved in the process of re-arranging the original song and, initially, in the direction of the orchestra, which was the Abbey Road Pops Orchestra. Peter Brown and Alan Parsons were the sound engineers. The suite was later renamed 'Atom Heart Mother', after the title of a newspaper article about a pregnant girl who was kept alive with the help of an atomic pacemaker. The song was recorded in July 1970 and was released on 2 October in the UK and 10 October in the US.

A few weeks later, on 11 December 1970, Robert Fripp's King Crimson released their third album, *Lizard*, a new chapter in a constantly evolving musical story that featured a suite on the whole of the second side. It was a mixture of different styles blended with improvisation and classical music. Fripp himself describes it in the 2009 *Lizard* reissue booklet as 'Lots of ideas, mostly presented simultaneously, very few of which work. There is one exception: the Bolero. The main theme, played on oboe by Robin Miller (co-principal oboist with the BBC Symphony Orchestra under Boulez at the time), is a gift. This is a melody which sustained me in difficult times.'

Before these Pink Floyd and King Crimson releases, Soft Machine managed to include as many as four long pieces on the same album. *Third*, released on 6 June 1970, is the perfect link between the psychedelic approach of the band's previous production and the jazz-rock feel that was typical of their future endeavours. Though the recording quality of *Third* is not optimal, it showcases the desire of the band to adopt the same free form of expression and improvisation that was part of Miles Davis' seminal albums *In A Silent Way* and *Bitches Brew*, coupled with the natural inclination towards sonic manipulation and pure experimentation that was pursued by the band members, especially by drummer Robert Wyatt.

Van der Graaf Generator's *Pawn Hearts* (October 1971) also hosts a long-form piece of music: a ten-part suite that fills a whole side of vinyl. The idea of widening the canvas was not something the band developed suddenly. The path started right from the first band album, 1969's *The Aerosol Grey Machine*, as part of a kind of linear progression. If we focus on the tracklists of the albums that the band released from 1969 to 1971, we can see how, as time goes by, the number of tracks included on every record decreases dramatically, switching from ten to three. What's more, as well as having a 20-minute suite on one side, *Pawn Hearts* features two long tracks on the other side. This is NOT quite the same approach as that of ELP or Caravan in the same year with their respective *Tarkus* and *In The Land Of Grey And Pink* albums, which paired one long-form piece – 'Tarkus' and 'Nine Feet Underground' – with some shorter tracks: *Tarkus* houses six short songs (none of them longer than four minutes) on side two and *In The Land Of Grey And Pink* showcases four shorter songs on side one. Another aspect worth noticing is that, as VdGG finally arrived at their classic four-piece lineup, dispensing with a bass player, their music started to become more and more complex. As we will see in the following chapters of this essay, on the album *Pawn Hearts*, the band – formed by Peter Hammill, Guy Evans, David Jackson and Hugh Banton – decided to push all the components to their limit: the writing of course, but also the playing and the recording process.

It is surely not my purpose to rank all the progressive rock albums that were released in the early 70s, but I cannot help pointing out that *Pawn Hearts* and the suite 'A Plague Of Lighthouse Keepers' saw the light some months before some other high influential records as *Close To The Edge* by Yes, *Foxtrot* by Genesis and *Thick As A Brick* by Jethro Tull, each one of them hosting at least one side-long piece. Is it possible, then, to define *Pawn Hearts* as a progenitor for such important works in the UK progressive rock scene? What's sure is that, in retrospect, the music press and critics regarded *Pawn Hearts* as the highest point in the band's catalogue and many believe it to be their finest album, a burst of incredible expressiveness. The music magazine *Rolling Stone* listed it at number 26 in its top 50 Progressive Rock Album poll back in 2015. Even the famous record producer John Anthony, who worked with Genesis, Queen and Roxy Music, claimed that *Pawn Hearts* is 'the most beautiful thing I've recorded in all my life.'

Actually, time has shown that *Pawn Hearts* was a unique event for the band and nearly a deviant one. The albums that precede it seem to be a gradual introduction, but the following ones detach from it in a clear and strong way. 'When we recorded Pawn Hearts,' later recalled Van der Graaf drummer Guy Evans, 'we experienced more real, heavy conflict between ourselves than we ever had done before. It produced a good result, but it placed the band in a difficult position. We just didn't know where to go from there.'

## From Six Bob Tour To New England Pop

Mannheim: rainy Saturday with no money nor friend...
Only Tequila can end the boredom.
Peter Hammill, 'German Overalls'

### January 1971

Tony Stratton Smith initially started out as a sports journalist. In the 1950s, after a stint at the *Birmingham Gazette*, he moved on to *The Daily Sketch*, thus becoming the youngest staff member on board. That meant 11 years of writing about cricket and football, even penning the odd article for *The Daily Express*. His passion for football prompted him to produce yearbooks, and it was during the 1962 World Cup in Chile that he met Brazilian Composer Antonio Carlos Jobim.

Hearing The Beatles' 'Love Me Do' is said to have sparked Tony's interest in music and all the peripheral activities surrounding its promotion. Let's make it clear, he wasn't in it for the bookkeeping, but his subsequent and often unlucky career as manager of bands such as The Koobas, The Nice, The Creation and The Bonzo Dog Doo Dah Band made it clear to him how important a serious record label was for a band's success. So, he took the only option he believed would work and founded his own label, which he decided to call Charisma. The first artists to be signed, together with The Nice, were Rare Bird (who, in 1969, had a smash hit single with *Sympathy*) and, of course, Van der Graaf Generator.

The symbiotic nature of Charisma, combining both record label and management as one rather than two separate entities as had previously been the norm, meant Stratton Smith had to be especially careful about the promotion of the artists under his wing. This meant sending them out to play as many gigs as they could manage to gain the maximum exposure. He realised this meant finding 'a different audience to the one which, every week, tuned in to *Top Of The Pops*', an alternative audience of kids and students quite possibly not hip to popular tastes and trends.

One of Tony Stratton Smith's most ingenious ideas was to promote a tour of several bands on the same label, a sort of travelling festival up and down England and Scotland. It wasn't a particularly novel idea in itself, except for the price of the ticket – a paltry six shillings, or Bob, if you prefer (basically just under a fiver in today's currency). Strat passed promotional duties over to John Smith and his son Tony, one of the youngest up-and-coming British promoters who had, after all, organised the first Beatles tour of the UK and talked The Who into bringing *Tommy* to the stage.

The legendary *Six Bob Tour* took off on 24 January 1971 at the renowned London Lyceum, where many so-called alternative concerts were being held at the time, and wound up on 13 February at The Winter Gardens in Bournemouth. The lineup would invariably be Lindisfarne, Genesis and Van der Graaf Generator, whom Stratton Smith had designated as headliners of the festival. Enormous success and sold-out venues ensued. In the February 1971 issue of *NME*, Roy Carr had this to report:

> Had I not chosen to travel up to Manchester on Saturday to witness the amazing scenes with my own eyes, I must truthfully admit that I would have been somewhat sceptical about all those stories of overflowing crowds who nightly have crammed the nation's major concert halls to see Van der Graaf Generator, Lindisfarne and Genesis. But the truth will out, and under the auspices of Charisma Records, this tour has proved to be about the most successful of its kind in nigh on two years. While many experienced promoters bemoan the fact that many over-priced, over-publicised artists are failing to consolidate their reputation in terms of box office returns, Charisma have succeeded in drawing capacity business in London, Birmingham, Bristol, Manchester and, most notably, Newcastle. It was here that well over 500 people had to be left out in the cold while 2,500 enthusiasts created scenes of almost unparalleled hysteria in the sanctum of the City Hall.

The *Six Bob Tour* was fundamental for the Generator's self-esteem. After releasing their second album and having reached number 47 in the national charts after selling about 15,000 copies, the band were anxious to see how well *H To He Who Am The Only One*, released just before the tour in December 1970, would do. Peter Hammill elaborated on this in *Melody Maker* on 27 March 1971:

> Before the tour, we'd never succeeded that way – you know, ovations and people getting up on their feet to us ... The price could have something to do with it, but then it can work the other way, with people thinking, 'Oh, we've only paid six bob, it can't be much good' … On the contrary, at nearly all the gigs, the audience have known most of the songs, and at some of them, there were guys sitting at the side of the stage singing along with everything.

Even the alchemy between the bands involved on the tour was successful, the joyous atmosphere eventually leading to a number of musical co-endeavours, such as Peter Hammill's collaborations with Ray Jackson and Rod Clements of Lindisfarne on his first solo outing, *Fool's Mate*, in the summer of 1971. In *Van der Graaf Generator: The Book*, John Anthony shares fond memories:

> It was great fun and the vibe was great. We all got on the coach and Van der Graaf Generator were in the back rolling joints, Lindisfarne had their crates of Newcastle Brown and Genesis sat there being uptight.

David Jackson has similar recollections:

> We'd hang out with the other bands and we used to watch each others' sets. With most shows, you don't even bother to leave the dressing room until it's your turn to play, but we used to go out and watch. The whole night would be a great vibe. At some shows, everyone would come out at the end to do things like 'After The Flood' or whatever.

No surprise then when it was announced that the *Six Bob Tour* would go on for an additional eight shows in April with the same lineup, except for the shows where Genesis or Lindisfarne would not be available and had to be replaced by Graham Bell and Arc. This, of course, underlined, once again, that the headliners were, in fact, Van der Graaf Generator, almost declaring which band the Charisma label saw as the most likely to break through, as Chris Welch remarked in the pages of *Melody Maker* in April 1971:

> Van der Graaf Generator are one of the more progressive bands currently storming around the nation to wild applause. They have had a long struggle for success and deserve the acclaim now coming their way. At Croydon, Fairfield Hall on Sunday, mass enthusiasm broke out for their moody but full-throated music. Brilliant organist Hugh Banton built up tension with his effective use of mystery chords, and particularly outstanding was the driving drums of Guy Evans, recalling the work of Robert Wyatt but looser and perhaps more flowing.

Regardless of the favourable reviews and the attention of the press, which peaked in May 1971 with VdGG sax player David Jackson surprisingly appearing on the cover of *Melody Maker*, the problem still seemed to be the less-than-biblical number of copies shifted by the band's third album, *H To He*. It had basically sold about as much as the band's previous offering. Charisma started to notice and was, justifiably, perplexed by this discrepancy between great gig attendance for the 'press darlings of the day' and the low record sales. Once again, Charisma decided that if English audiences were not ready for Van der Graaf, then they had to look overseas, principally Holland and Germany, which seemed to be particularly favourable to certain forms of music.

Stratton Smith, building on the success in the UK, sent some of his bands abroad under the banner of the *New London Pop Tour*. The lineup consisted of Van der Graaf, Audience and Jackson Heights (the titular Lee Jackson being the ex-bass player of the Nice), and they were scheduled on a 17-gig tour of Germany.

### May 1971

In my book *Van der Graaf Generator – La Biografia Italiana*, I looked at how the band's relationship with Italy, which began with their highly successful tour in February 1972, would leave a profound mark, for good or bad, on the

Generator's history. The 1971 German tour would also leave a mark, albeit not commercially, as it was very underwhelming in that sense, but more decidedly on a personal and artistic level. The brutal alienation experienced by Hammill, Banton, Evans and Jackson during their three-week Teutonic pilgrimage would change the way the band wrote together and led, in a very short space of time, to the appearance of *Pawn Hearts*.

Characterised by very minimal organisation, the *New London Pop Tour* kicked off on 1 May 1971 in Essen and came to an end amidst myriad problems 20 days later in Berlin. Charisma, in an attempt to cut costs, let a logistics company, Kosmos Reisen (still active to this day), handle the tour, cooping the bands up in a van for the full period of the tour and for what seemed like an endless series of road trips in an increasingly uncomfortable situation. As if that weren't enough, the financial side of matters was handled far from impeccably. The musicians were not paid after each gig but were forced to wait for a Charisma representative to come over from the UK with their pay. This meant that the bands were broke most of the time, as none of them had bothered to bring any cash along from home. Peter Hammill spoke of such frustrations during an interview with Jonathan Barnett in 1976: 'It was on that tour that the collective brain went. Three weeks in an ice cream van. Not being paid any money, and when we were paid in dollars, we couldn't change it into Deutschmarks.' Guy Evans goes into further detail in *The Book*: 'We were going around on this tiny little bus with all the bands in it, staying in some really appalling hotels ... really the pits. Nobody had any money; the money was always supposed to be arriving.' Money concerns were also outlined by Hugh Banton during a Sid Smith interview in February 2022:

> On the earlier tours in Germany in 1970 or 1971, we were out of funds. Wages that had been sent weren't turning up and so we'd basically starve. It wasn't like now, where you have a hotel paid for and food backstage. There wasn't anything like that then. It was a nightmare.

Without even the necessary change in their pockets to make a phone call home, all that was left for the band to do was carry on playing. Even that was a bit of a problem for the band; on top of the inevitable accumulated sense of frustration and tiredness which seeped out of the band's shows, the VdGG set didn't sit well with the Germans and, amidst the feedback and general cacophony, it was possible to make out quite a bit of heckling and booing sent in the band's general direction.

The extent of the German troubles would reverberate for a while to come in Hammill's songwriting. The leader of VdGG poured his vitriol into a song ('German Overalls') featured on his second solo album released in 1973, *Chameleon In The Shadows Of The Night*. The song title alludes to the majestic sound of the German national anthem, 'Deutschland Uber Alles': 'Germany over all' and the more down-to-earth 'overalls' worn by modern factory workers. The fatigue of the latter was what our artists must have felt during their *New London Pop* experience. But the song was to be even more explicit:

Rathaus-keepers and traffic police,
Middle-aged maids with rotting teeth,
Industrial magazines and old Sunday Times:
Reading material/bleeding lines.
What are we doing here?

We're at the mercy of the Kosmos tour,
Making a pilgrimage to the German Lourdes...
But we're still crippled here.

Furthermore, in his book of lyrics, poems and short stories, *Killers, Angels And Refugees*, published in 1974, the author pens an epistolary tale entitled 'Audi', in which Peter, writing from Mannheim, tells a female pen-friend all about his devastating experience in Germany, sparing very little in the way of detail. Such an experience would have wrecked any other band, but for our heroes, it would only spur them on to greater heights. In the van that housed our band, Hammill got to work on the lyrics for 'A Plague Of Lighthouse Keepers'. The index of *Killers, Angels And Refugees* states the date and place of composition of the lyrics next to the song titles, and so we learn that *Plague* lyrics were written in 'Fawley Road, a Kosmos – Reisen coach in mid-Germany, Worth 1971'. In the same van, the four-piece discussed, with feverish intensity, the shape the new compositions would take for the next VdGG album. All agreed that the sound had to be unique and had to present something not yet attempted so as to prove to the world, after so many disappointments, that there really was something special about their art.

# The Haunted Palace

> I really loved how things were going at the time ... For the most part, we were completely freaked out.
> Guy Evans

## June 1971

Once the daring *New London Pop Tour* with Audience and Jackson Heights had been put aside, and after completing two more dates in Switzerland at the end of May, Van der Graaf Generator finally had the chance to focus on the completion of their fourth album. Throughout June and part of July 1971, the band moved to Tony Stratton Smith's imposing country house in Crowborough, a small town in Sussex, about 40 miles away from London, with the aim of perfecting the new songs and preparing them for the recording sessions that would take place later at Trident Studios in London. Both rehearsals and recordings took place in a decidedly chaotic and fragmented way, mainly due to the fact that the band were called to perform a series of concerts in the same period. In fact, Van der Graaf had ten dates in Great Britain in June (including the famous Reading Festival, along with Colosseum, Osibisia, Medicine Head and Rory Gallagher) and 15 more in the next month. Moreover, on 10 June 1971, Hammill, Evans, Banton and Jackson recorded four tunes for the BBC program *Sounds Of The Seventies*, two of which – 'Man-Erg' and 'Theme One' – were still unreleased, proving that the band were already ahead with the songwriting. This is also confirmed by the fact that, before starting the rehearsals with the rest of the band, Hammill provided a substantial preview of the material to the producer, John Anthony, who was charged once again with co-ordinating the sound recordings, as he outlined in *The Book*:

> When we were going to do *Pawn Hearts*, Peter invited me down to Worth and we just sat there for the whole day with lots of Guinness, red wine and spliffs. In between sets of badminton on his lawn, he played me the entire album on his acoustic guitar and piano – the whole album.

In a phone interview while touring Germany, later published in the May issue of *Record Mirror,* David Jackson stated that the new album would have been released in July and that it would have been a double LP, given the large amount of available material.

So, in June 1971, the majestic Luxford House became the perfect scenario for the sedimentation of the psychedelic drift Van der Graaf Generator had experienced in the previous months. It is said that the old building, surrounded by a wide garden, was populated by strange and mysterious presences. At the time, in an interview published in *Melody Maker*, Hammill revealed that the band had already visited the house during the making of their third album, *H To He Who Am The Only One*, to listen to the album premix along with Stratton-Smith and that, during the listening, paintings kept falling from the walls and rolling onto the floor by themselves. Stratton-Smith elaborated further on the G2 Definitive Genesis website:

> It was a lovely old Tudor house, which was in the centre spread of Van der Graaf's *Pawn Hearts* album cover, and there was a joke about the house being haunted, the sort of house with 16th-century timbers that appeared to have very good vibes for musicians. Many have worked and stayed there – Neil Diamond, Leonard Cohen, Van der Graaf, Bert Jansch, Bob Johnson, Mike Nesmith.

The use of acid and cannabis by the band during the rehearsals did not do anything else but cast a wider aura of mystery on the austere location, as outlined by Guy Evans in *The Book*:

> It was a very spooky house, like the houses in every Hammer horror movie you've seen. It was a large Tudor mansion with very old, twisting wooden floors. It's very dark and low and mysterious ... quite good!

In *The Book*, John Anthony shares similar recollections:

> There was a vibe there in one room where there was a painting above the fireplace with these eyes – it isn't amazing; its eyes follow you everywhere! It's one of those old clichés! It's like a Peter Cook and Dudley Moore sketch – it's really only art if the eyes follow you everywhere when you're in the room; that's how you can tell a truly great portrait. Well, I did see something weird there. Mind you, I had done a lot of acid!

As we will see, the old house also left a tangible presence in the new album's artwork. It was immortalised behind the four musicians in the picture included in the gatefold packaging of the vinyl. Curiously, in July, as soon as Van der Graaf moved to Trident Studios in London to record the new songs, Genesis took their place in the house to start rehearsing for the *Nursery Cryme* album, experiencing the same singular events which had happened to their label mates, detailed by Phil Collins on the G2 website:

> I'm sure the house was haunted. There were some weird vibes. There was a picture with eyes that followed you everywhere and other strange things. But by that time, I was hip to what the band were doing and I enjoyed it.

When they entered Luxford House, Van der Graaf had already arranged some songs that were just waiting to be refined. In fact, the band had already performed 'Man-Erg' live before the summer, along with the instrumental 'Theme One' and, as already mentioned, they played these last two songs during the 10 June 1971 BBC session: a hint that the band had already assimilated them. Given the length of the songs, which were ideally intended to fill a whole side of vinyl, the four musicians had nothing to do but devote themselves to the elaboration of the material that would form the second side of the new album. However, the various members of the band had decidedly opposing ideas about this point: given the size of the first side, the organist Hugh Banton had expected that the album was going to be completed with a series of shorter and more immediate pieces. Peter Hammill instead had something completely different in mind. According to Hammill, it was time to give a final shape to that long and mysterious composition with which he started to confront himself while travelling through Germany with the others aboard the tiny bus. In his view, that composition would occupy the whole B-side of the new album. Hugh Banton detailed his response to Hammill's suggestion to Sid Smith in 2022:

> At the time, people forgot that our career was going into a slow decline. We'd had great press reviews of *The Least We Can Do Is Wave To Each Other* and then slightly less so for *H To He Who Am The Only One*. Our contemporaries, like Genesis and Lindisfarne, all had numbers that would get people up on their feet cheering. We didn't have anything like that. I think there was a feeling at the time that we had to have more of these kinds of numbers; otherwise, we would lose the meagre audience we'd got. So when 'A Plague Of Lighthouse Keepers' was being presented to us, we were wondering if this was quite the way we should be going. I thought, 'Urgh, what is this? We can't even play this thing!'

In the *Charisma Years* booklet, Peter Hammill talked about the process of recording 'A Plague Of Lighthouse Keepers':

> All the parts of what became 'A Plague Of Lighthouse Keepers' were conceived before we entered the studio – at least in my mind, they were. I have to say that these parts needed a great deal of writing manipulation and linking by the others in the group. It was recorded in small parts and we didn't know how the piece would turn out until we got down to mixing it.

The fulfilment of the 'A Plague Of Lighthouse Keepers' suite represented a moment of great conflict and fracture within the band. The other three musicians were not convinced at all about this song, nor about recording it. While Hammill was usually able to make his 'fellow adventurers' listen to his new songs on the piano or on the acoustic guitar before involving them in the arrangement, in this case, there was no structure at all. There was just a series of fragments. Hammill had not even written some of these fragments, but they were out-and-out Jackson or Evans or Banton micro-compositions that Hammill had picked up during soundchecks or rehearsals. He kept these

**pieces somewhere in his mind, and during the German tour, he had begun putting them together and linking them through a series of lyrics that could somehow tell a unified story. In *The Book*, Hugh Banton made the cause of his reservations clear:**

> The problem was that Peter had all these bits completed but evidently expected us to figure out how to join them together! He just had all these fragments, so that's why we kind of went, 'What?'

**Guy Evans had this to say on the matter in *The Book*:**

> I think Hugh would feel more responsibility for its coherence because a lot of the harmonic movement of everything was in his hands. A classic conversation between Peter and Hugh would be, 'Okay, we've got to get from this section to this section. How are we going to do it?' Usually, it would be up to Hugh to figure out a way of transitioning.

**Peter Hammill summarised proceedings during an interview with *Fresh Fruit* magazine in 1976:**

> We did have a complete schism, and the whole thing nearly fell apart. In the end, everybody came over to Worth and got drunk – the usual sort of Van der Graaf resolution – and we decided to go on and do 'Lighthouse Keepers'. As the evening went on, we patched things up and thought that we'd give it a go. So we went back to rehearsing it, and suddenly, we were storming along. By the weekend, we had it all figured out.

**With its 23-minute length and its ten sections, 'A Plague Of Lighthouse Keepers' was to remain a matter of discussion and debate, even after its release. The position of the British press towards the new album and the long suite, in particular, included much criticism. Since Hammill was personally involved, he did not hesitate to openly defend the choices made in a 1972 *Sounds* interview:**

> To me, the album is 'A Plague Of Lighthouse Keepers' – the other things aren't unimportant but they are pretty much follow-ons to the other songs. 'Lighthouse Keepers' is something more, and it's what interested me more about the album. I don't know if it comes over to other people or not, but there's a lot there ... it runs on three levels simultaneously and I worked on it for months and months ... We did have an awful lot of hassle about the whole thing – whether we wanted to do it, how to do it, whether it was right to do it ... it's very difficult to talk about it because it was such a traumatic thing to do altogether. I regard it as being what we've been leading up to. 'Lighthouse Keepers' is a solid peak.

## July 1971

In mid-July, Van der Graaf Generator moved from Luxford House to Trident Studios in London to start recording the songs that were going to form the album on a 16-track machine. At the time, Trident was among the best-known recording studios in England thanks to the quality of the machinery and the skills of the sound engineers. Elton John recorded several albums at Trident, as did David Bowie, Genesis, Lindisfarne and Queen, just to mention some of the most famous names. Aware of the commitment all this would take, John Anthony decided to involve four sound engineers in the recording sessions: Robin Cable, David Hentschel, Ken Scott and Roy Thomas Baker (although the latter is not featured in the album credits, his name features on the 'A Plague Of Lighthouse Keepers' master tape cover as part of the studio engineers team who took care of recording the suite). As Anthony had guessed, the band did not just perform the songs as developed in the previous weeks, but they adopted an extremely creative approach, even during recording and mixing, as outlined by Hugh Banton in *The Book*:

> We were all buzzing with things we wanted to do. *Pawn Hearts* is full of some pretty mad stuff: psychedelic razors, sound effects, backwards tapes ... we wanted to try everything. Every time someone had an idea, it was like, 'Yeah, let's do it.' There wouldn't be five minutes gone by without someone coming up with something insane to do, and John Anthony would find a way to do it.

### *Pawn Hearts* recordings calendar

| | |
|---|---|
| 12 July 1971 | 'Man Erg' part 1 |
| 12 July 1971 | 'Man Erg' part 2 |
| 12 July 1971 | 'Man Erg' part 3 |
| 15 July 1971 | 'W' (named as 'Double You') |
| 15 July 1971 | 'Theme One' |
| 19 July 1971 | 'Lemmings' part 1 |
| 20 July 1971 | 'Lemmings' part 2 |
| 20 July 1971 | 'Eyewitness' part 1 |
| 20 July 1971 | 'Pictures/Lighthouse' |
| 20 July 1971 | 'Eyewitness' part 2 |
| 20 July 1971 | 'SHM' |
| 21 July 1971 | 'Presence Of The Night' |
| 21 July 1971 | 'Kosmos Tours' |
| 3 August 1971 | '(Custard's) Last Stand' |
| 3 August 1971 | 'The Clot Thickens' |
| 3 August 1971 | 'Land's End' |
| 3 August 1971 | 'We Go Now' |

From the sound point of view, there are actually some very particular choices. For example, for many years, I asked myself what the elusive 'psychedelic razor' was, which was attributed to Hugh Banton in the credits, along with some other conventional instruments such as Hammond, Farfisa, Mellotron, ARP synthesiser, bass and piano. It must be said that in the 1970s, album credits were often full of tricks and jokes that alluded to facts, characters or situations that had somehow characterised the creation of an album, often only fully understood by those involved. So, at the time *Pawn Hearts* was released, the presence of a 'psychedelic razor' in the back cover notes was not given much importance. Then, a deeper analysis seemed to lead the razor back to Banton's artistic skills: maybe he had collaborated with John Anthony to cut and assemble, in the right sequence, all the small pieces of tape on which the various segments of the 'A Plague Of Lighthouse Keepers' suite were separately recorded?

We know now that this referred to what is contained in the 'noisy' section of the opening track, 'Lemmings', and more specifically to the part from 4.56 to 5.16, which is used as an introduction to the section called 'Cog'. In this short period of time, first in the distance and then in a very strong and prominent way, we can hear some cavernous and distorted sounds that perhaps imitate the powering up of huge industrial machines. Not surprisingly, a little later, the lyrics speak of 'cog-wheels that grind man', a perfect symbol of progress attacking our lives (Gentle Giant used the image of a mechanical wheel in the song 'Cogs In Cogs' from 1974's *The Power And The Glory* album). A person being like a cog – meaning a person who has become a small part of a machine that they cannot control – is a common metaphor in English. In fact, being a cog is very similar indeed to being a pawn: a small part of a larger thing.

Peter Hammill and Hugh Banton assembled the short section to somehow connect the first part (from 0.00 to 4.56) and the second part (from 5.16 to end) of the song. In fact, 'Lemmings' presented a very clear break between the two parts, recorded separately on two different multitrack tapes. According to Peter Hammill in *A Musical Guide To Pawn Hearts:*

> We had to bridge these two sections and Hugh Banton and I went off to bring in our own bits of concrete to do the job: his razor (literally a varispeed electric razor) and my guitar with (metal) bottleneck, first slowly sliding up before a fast descent. I think, though, a heavy compressed acoustic rather than an electric.

Hugh Banton takes up the story in *The Book*:

> Peter and I had gone to our parents' homes in Derby and Torquay, respectively. We both had reel-to-reel tape recorders with us at our homes and, coincidentally, both started messing around making electronic tapes. So,

> I took my tape out of the capstan so I could rotate it by hand. I found that I could put it in record mode and get it to rewind at the same time, so it would record at about 200 ips and so on, backwards and forwards. I was recording a battery shaver, and it was just this *incredible* noise.

**COGS introduction tracks list**

| | | |
|---|---|---|
| 1 | Peter's Noise | Stereo |
| 2 | Peter's Noise | Stereo |
| 3 | Hugh's Noise | |
| 4 | Hugh's Noise | |
| 5 | Hugh's Noise | |
| 6 | Hugh's Noise 75 IPS | |

The two musicians' work is correctly included in the album credits: the slide guitar appears among the instruments played by Hammill, while the use of the 'psychedelic razor' is attributed to Banton. The five fragments recorded by Hammill (one stereo track) and Banton (four mono tracks) were transferred on a new multitrack tape – labelled as 'Cog Introduction' – at Trident Studios and then mixed to get the desired effect.

According to the master tapes tracklists, the recording of *Pawn Hearts* took place between 12 July and 3 August 1971, but as occurred during the Crowborough stay, the sessions did not happen continuously, so the band were not based in the studio uninterruptedly for three months, as you might imagine. Peter Hammill explained this in the *Pawn Hearts* 2005 remastered CD booklet:

> In those days, we recorded over a long calendar period, but the actual sessions weren't long. We were on tight budgets and recording was sandwiched in between live dates. We would be allowed six hours in the middle of the night to record. When we recorded 'W', we had driven all the way from Twickenham directly to Trident Studios in Soho. We tumbled out of the van, went into the studio, recorded the track and were finally able to go home.

Once the recordings of the various tracks were completed, the mixing of the album was managed in a very original way. As electronic mixers were not available yet – starting from 1975, the mix automation allowed the mixing console to remember the audio engineer's adjustment of faders during the editing process and repeat them automatically at the time of mixing – all four members of the band were called to actively participate in the proceedings, as outlined by John Anthony in *The Book*:

> The mixing sessions were fantastic. I would direct it and it's hand-mixed – no computers. We would set the basic mix up, then we would give all four

of them key things to do – punch that up there or move that knob back to that little china-graph pencil mark – and so it was like an octopus with as many as 200 'moves' in each section of the mix. The band were great because they could do it.

Peter Hammill was a little more concise in his summary of it to *Mojo* in 2007: 'The mixing, which often involved six pairs of hands, was effectively a live performance.'

As expected, the greatest effort was dedicated to the recording and mixing of the suite. To manage all the effects assigned to the various tracks, such as delay, phaser and several repetitions, the band were forced to use every single apparatus available at the studio. At one point, the band were even permitted by Anthony to record – in a monophonic version – a whopping 16 different songs from their back catalogue, one for each of the tracks available on the recording machine. Playing them all together created a brief moment of total cacophony within one of the 'A Plague Of Lighthouse Keepers' sections, which is 'Kosmos Tours'.

The story of the finalisation of the long passage, taken from a conversation in October 1976 between Hammill, Evans and Bob Anderson, editor of the American magazine *Fresh Fruit*, is definitely unique, both in the introduction and in conclusion, with Banton and Anthony left alone inside the Trident Studios with the challenge of connecting many pieces of tape to each other in some way.

Guy Evans: It wasn't continuous. Not in sequence at all. We recorded 'Lighthouse Keepers' in about eight or nine parts. It got to a point where we couldn't remember what we'd done, and at one point, we managed to wipe the master twice.

Peter Hammill: Twice in an evening! A real devilish mix, and we'd mixed away for hours, and then David turned around just to play it back and he just wiped one second. So, 'All right, it's no good freaking out, we've just got to do it again.' So we did it again. Two hours later, he turns round, ready to play it back, another half second's worth. 'No, all right, no good freaking out, we've just got to do it again.' So, it was strange ... I just decided crazily, for some reason, to do a solo gig again at a folk club across London.

Guy Evans: Dave, Peter and I went down to this little pub and left Hugh doing all the edits and cross-fades.

Peter Hammill: At that point, we knew exactly where everything was going and exactly what each edit and cross-fade was going to be, but it was a question of doing it exactly right. He did it, and, of course, they'd just

> heard each section and the marrying passages. And then we came back from the gig, and it was ready finally, about two in the morning, for the first time, never having heard 'Lighthouse Keepers' the way it was on vinyl. It had never been continuous. We'd never played it before. For about four to five months, it was hovering in the air around us, and then finally, in a rush, it was there, and that was really amazing. At that point, I remember thinking I could die then, after that. I thought I could die completely.

Given the difficulties the band encountered in completing the *Pawn Hearts* recordings and mix, thinking that the work could actually have been even more complex can bring a smile. According to Peter Hammill in the *Pawn Hearts* 2005 remastered CD booklet:

> The original idea was to make that record a double album that would consist of the tracks we all know as *Pawn Hearts* but would also include three individual instrumental tracks by Guy, Hugh and David. The other idea was to record a few songs that had been live staples of the show for some time but were now getting a bit long in the tooth. We thought we could show what the live versions of that material had been like, so we recorded 'Killer', 'Darkness' and 'Squid/Octopus', which had basically been played live as far back as the days when Keith Ellis was in the band. However, ultimately, Charisma Records felt that it wasn't appropriate for us to release a double album and they vetoed the live studio recordings and the solo tracks by Guy, David and Hugh.

In *The Book*, Hugh Banton appeared clueless regarding the matter:

> I can't remember why *Pawn Hearts* was not released as a double album. It was probably that Charisma needed to get the thing released and we hadn't finished it. Also, we weren't too sure about the live side.

Whereas Guy Evans gave a diplomatic view in *The Book*:

> My feeling is that, although that seemed a logical thing to do at the time of making the record – one album of *Pawn Hearts* the way it is, half of the second album with these solo tracks and the other half the band live – I now think, retrospectively, that *Pawn Hearts* as it is *and* the solo tracks are fairly groundbreaking ... and the live stuff actually belongs to a previous era.

While understanding Evans' and Banton's doubts, it is quite exciting to listen today to the live version of a song like 'Octopus', which miraculously emerged from the Virgin cellars and was readily inserted as a bonus track on the 2005 remastered version of *H To He*. The 15-minute blast that floods the listener actually gives a clear idea of the state of the band at that precise moment in 1971. This was a band that, even in concert, were trying to go beyond the edge of their technical and expressive abilities. Apart from the brief introductory section of 'Octopus' that involved him on the acoustic guitar, Hammill was exclusively limited to singing, maximising the sonic impact of the band's atypical lineup, devoid of both bass and guitar, with Hugh Banton able to draw completely new sounds out of his customised E-112 Hammond organ.

Tony Banks, in the introduction to the booklet within *The Box* (2000), had the opportunity to emphasise the fact that, at the time, when thinking of VdGG, one of the first images that came to his mind was surely that of Hugh Banton with his head stuck inside the organ, desperately trying to run the complex effects system, distortion and fuzz box which it was implemented with. This always-evolving mechanism led Banton to design and assemble his own personal organ, which he managed to complete only at the end of 1976, shortly before his departure from the band.

If the side containing the old songs played live in the studio demonstrated the cohesion and harmony of the four Generators, along with the undoubted ability of the band to fully express its potential in a live context, the side destined to display Banton's, Evans' and Jackson's solo compositions entered some rather different areas, which were a subject of interest and research for the three musicians. 'Angle Of Incidents', created and then recorded by the drummer with the saxophonist's collaboration, is an almost five-minute instrumental piece focused on the exaltation of rhythm and percussion. Various drums, cymbals, percussion and timpani patterns overlap within the song, some of which are played backwards until the break in the middle of the track, during which we can hear the sound of breaking glass. Guy Evans recalled the experience in *The Charisma Years* booklet:

> We were the first band to record on 16-track at Trident. Fortunately for us, this also translated into a brilliantly encouraging attitude to our own experiments. I was allowed to festoon the stairwell with expensive microphones hooked up to every available effect and drop a bunch of neon tubes (belonging to Trident!) from top to bottom so that they would explode. Robin Cable didn't bat an eyelid!

Throughout the whole song, Evans' slowed or reversed voice is also present, marking several times the sequence 'Five – Four – Three – Two – One – Zero'. In the closing, the sequence changes to 'Five – Four – Three – Two – One – END', and just after that, we can hear Evans' final comment thanking the sound engineer, Robin Cable ('Thank you, Robin, that would be fine').

Banton's contribution materialised in the six-minute 'Diminutions', an instrumental composition consisting of several overlapped and filtered organ tracks that seem to develop the wonderful modulation section of 'A Plague Of Lighthouse Keepers', which acts as a liaison between 'Pictures/Lighthouse' and the second part of 'Eyewitness'. Recently, Banton released a sequel to the song, titled 'Diminutions 2', on his Bandcamp page and defined the original track as 'an abstract impressionist piece, created in the main by a technical collaboration between my somewhat modified Hammond stage organ and the latest effects and processes available to us at Trident Studios.' For his part, David Jackson wrote a multi-part piece called 'Agamemnon Archimedes Agnostic', to which Hammill contributed a Greek text that was apparently inspired by anti-fascism. A segment of the lyric is quoted in an interview with Hammill and Evans, published in *OD Magazine* in 1976:

Archimedes Agamemnon agnostic
Now the Blackshirts are coming here
Live in freedom not in Fear

However, the song was never recorded, although the composition had actually been completed on the piano. In 2005, during the remastering process of the band's catalogue, the first two songs were miraculously recovered and included in the *Pawn Hearts* reissue, while Jackson's song was 'replaced' by the short 'Ponker's Theme', a delicate 90-second jazzy interlude in which the sax melody is complemented with bass, drums and piano.

In retrospect, the idea of dedicating an entire side of the second LP to solo compositions by Van der Graaf without Hammill appears to reveal the personal dynamics among the musicians in the band. Hammill had initially taken the load of the whole artistic aspect, composing the music and writing the lyrics, and had just released his first solo album, so at some point, the others probably felt the need to step into the spotlight.

Once the *Pawn Hearts* concept idea vanished, the inspiration of providing a showcase to the three musicians materialised unexpectedly just a few months later, in February 1972, when Van der Graaf Generator released the 'Theme One'/'W' single – much to the public's surprise – which centred on Banton's, Evans' and Jackson's reinterpretation (without Hammill) of the famous Radio One theme song, composed by Sir George Martin in 1967. It was a brilliant gimmick that allowed the single to be quite popular (especially in Italy) so that when, in the same year, Charisma decided to release *Pawn Hearts* in the United States, 'Theme One' was inserted onto the A-side in a rather bumpy way, between 'Lemmings' and 'Man-Erg', creating a strong gap between the two tracks because of its jaunty gait. When Peter Hammill learnt about this decision, he hit the roof.

## Into The Maelstrom Of The Memory

> By this point, we had gone beyond the borders of the finite, where we have been ever since. And sometimes, in the course of making that album, it was hard to find even the most tenuous connection with ... reality ... normality.
> Peter Hammill

Ricardo Odriozola is a Spanish violin player, composer, orchestra leader and teacher at the Grieg Academy in Bergen, Norway. In 2007, he tried to deconstruct and rebuild the whole of *Pawn Hearts*, producing a musical guide that also included the score for the album. The guide was presented and explained to the Italian fans in Guastalla that same year during a series of meetings held by the Peter Hammill and Van der Graaf Generator Study Group. It's a fascinating piece of work – released with the help of David Jackson and Hugh Banton – though sometimes it may get a bit difficult to read, especially when it comes to the musical notation. Anyway, Odriozola's essay will be a solid and essential reference point to our *Pawn Hearts* analysis, together with the notes to the translation of the lyrics from English to Italian that Marco Olivotto edited to be included in the *Dark Figures Running* book, published in 2005 by the Peter Hammill and Van der Graaf Generator Study Group. I suggest that you read this chapter while listening to the album tracks.

### **Side A** (22.01)

**'Lemmings (Including Cog)'** (11.23)

The album opens unusually with a fade-in lasting about 15 seconds. From the dark, an acoustic guitar arpeggio appears, played by Hammill, before the other instruments join in. Oddly, *Pawn Hearts* is the last Van der Graaf Generator album to feature an acoustic guitar.

The sound of wind, as already featured on *The Least We Can Do*'s opening track – 'Darkness (11/11)' – can be heard for 20 seconds before the introduction of a voice. The protagonist of the story outlines a dramatic and cruel scene taking place in front of him:

> I stood alone upon the highest cliff-top,
> Looked down, around, and all that I could see
> Were those that I would dearly love to share with
> Crashing on quite blindly to the sea...
> I tried to ask what game this was
> But knew I would not play it:
> The voice, as one, as no one, came to me...

Those who are running towards the sea, with whom the protagonist would like to interact, are, in fact, the lemmings: little rodents that live in the Arctic and northern side of Europe. In the 1970s, it was common to think that these animals regularly committed suicide, jumping from high cliffs and rushing into the sea. However, Odriozola clears up how this legend was fuelled by a 1958 Walt Disney documentary: a dozen of these little animals were transported onto a cliff and forced to jump into a river to ensure that the suicide theory could be documented. The impact of the film on the collective imagination is also proved by the Amon Düül II album *Tanz Der Lemminge* (The Lemmings Dance), which was released a few months before *Pawn Hearts.*

As the drums crash in and the organ goes into a chromatic climax, the first minute of the song is over – a rise of the curtain that immediately catches the attention of the listener. Both Odriozola and Dean Carter, who, in 1990, penned an extended analysis of the album for VdGG fanzine *Pilgrims*, highlight how this part is not repeated during the rest of the song. The initial crescendo opens the road for the main riff of the song, played by David Jackson's sax. It is a four-note sequence, quite martial in sound.

Now, together with the riff, it's the lemmings' turn to answer the call of the protagonist:

We have looked upon the heroes and they are found wanting;
We have looked hard across the land but we can see no dawn;
We have now dared to sear the sky but we are still bleeding;
We are drawing near to the cliffs,
Now we can hear the call.

This section, comprising the main riff and some variations (the 'first theme' according to Odriozola), lasts about another minute and leads to a harmonic development that requires our attention. The organ, initially contributing to the beginning's ominous atmosphere, now gives a brief sense of peace and satisfaction through its more mellow and positive-sounding major key change (1.58 – 2.05). Significantly, this switch in mood immediately follows the lemmings' line, 'What course is there left but to die?'. The lemmings' question to the protagonist, coupled with the major key change, acts like a tempting Pied Piper call, difficult to resist.

The whole section is then played another time (2.06 – 3.37) as the lemmings continue to pursue their choice of death:

For if the sky is seeded death
What is the point in catching breath? Expel it.

What cause is there left but to die
In searching of something we're really not too sure of?

Now is the right time to ask: who are the lemmings and what are they meant to represent in Hammill's writing? According to Dean Carter in *Pilgrims #9*, the rodents running towards self-destruction embody the downside of the Love Generation, a term often associated with the countercultural movement of the late 1960s, particularly the Summer of Love in San Francisco, that challenged traditional values and institutions, embracing free love, drug use (especially psychedelics) and a rejection of materialism:

> By 1971, after all, the hippie and New Age movements had lost momentum, the dream was over and the whole 1960s adventure seemed somehow to have crumbled, and very largely from within. All that optimism and creativity had turned into self-destruction, nihilism.

A quieter moment is the prologue to what Odriozola calls 'the second theme'. It is significant that, after listening to the lemmings' gruesome desires, the protagonist is now allowed to express his thoughts in response:

I know our ends may be soon but why do you make them sooner?
Time may finally prove only the living move here and
No life lies in the quicksand.

The vocal melody is introduced by the acoustic guitar in the open tuning of D G C F A C. An acoustic guitar in the left channel plays the melody, with another in the right channel initially playing strummed harmonics before resorting to the melody. When the whole band join in (4.00), the theme is repeated once with vocals and then again without vocals (4.20), except for three impressive shouts. Hammill manages to reach a high F, one octave and a half from the central C note – an impressive show of Hammill's vocal range.

Once again, the musical flow slows down before coming to a halt as we reach the notorious noisy piece – achieved by overlapping Hammill's home-made sonic experimentations with Banton's (the aforementioned 'Psychedelic Razor') – which introduces the section entitled 'Cog' (5.17). This part of the song, lasting slightly more than a minute, is based on the savage alternation between Jackson's chromatic double horn riff, over which Hammill howls his desperation, and a musical break whose atmosphere is completely antithetical, featuring only acoustic guitar arpeggios and Hammill's singing, which is extremely delicate. The protagonist seems to be now embracing the nihilistic proposition of the lemmings while abandoning all hope of redemption in what Carter describes as 'a sort of mechanical hell, a Boschian vision':

**Above:** Le Tout-Paris. Van der Graaf outside the Bataclan on 18 March 1972. The concert was filmed for French TV show *Pop 2. (Herman Parmentier)*

**Below:** When in Rome! Hammill on stage at the Charisma Festival on 22 January 1973. *(Emilio Maestri)*

1. Napoleon
2. John Lennon
3. A king/emperor
4. A guy carrying someone on his shoulders. Someone said it could be the killer (referencing the 'Man-Erg' lyrics) carrying his victim on his shoulders.
5. (The coronation of) Charlemagne
6. There has been speculation that this was a portrait of Robert J. Van de Graaf, but that was not confirmed by the artist, who said that it's just 'a British politician'.
7. A musketeer
8. A sailor
9. Winston Churchill
10. An astronaut. Neil Armstrong was the 'quintessential hero' at the time when the album was released. It's interesting how this figure is a mixture of collage and painting.
11. Julius Caesar
12. William Shakespeare
13. A soldier from the Queen's Royal Guard Of The Yeomen Of The Guard

14. A man with an axe. It could be the executioner or, again, the killer.
15. Jesus Christ
16. A cricket player.
17. A man dressed as a referee. Paul Whitehead appointed him simply as 'Mr. Average'.
18. An alien. Whitehead explained:

> That's a very famous little character called Eagle who was in English comics when we were kids. It was a weekly series. There was a character called Dan Dare and it was a very English, 1950s idea of what space travel would be like. They're all very British and honourable, right? And the villain was this guy called the Mekon. He floated around because his brain was so big that his body couldn't stand up.

It's been noted how the alien is one of the few characters that is not caught in a pawn ...

19. A policeman floating into space on a little boat, sustained by some balloons, much like an aerostat.

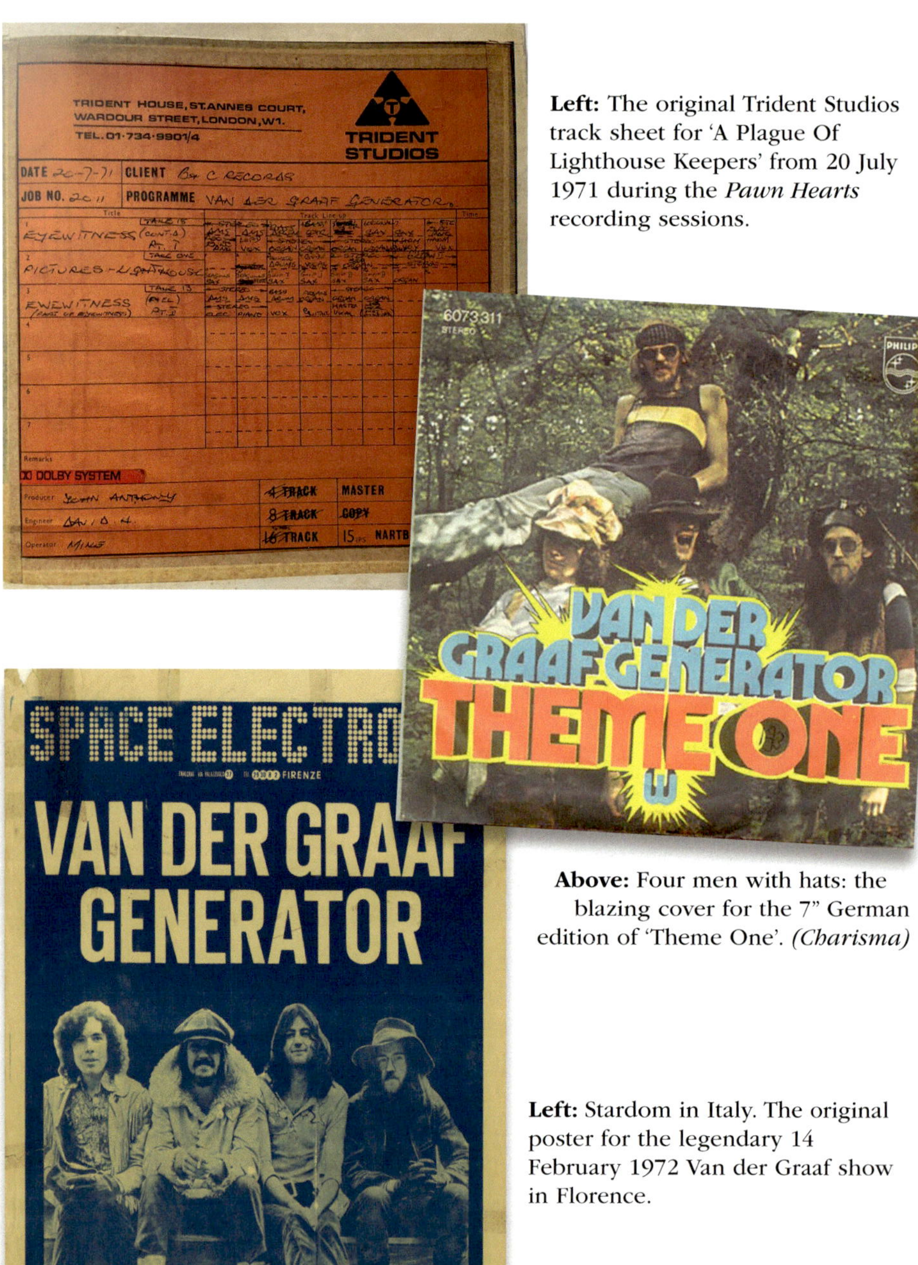


**Left:** The original Trident Studios track sheet for 'A Plague Of Lighthouse Keepers' from 20 July 1971 during the *Pawn Hearts* recording sessions.

**Above:** Four men with hats: the blazing cover for the 7" German edition of 'Theme One'. *(Charisma)*

**Left:** Stardom in Italy. The original poster for the legendary 14 February 1972 Van der Graaf show in Florence.

**Left:** Van der Graaf are back! Italian magazine *Ciao 2001* celebrated two reunion gigs in Italy in the May 1973 issue.

**Below:** The Generator's engine. Guy Evans (born on 17 June 1947) on stage with Van der Graaf in Italy in 1972.

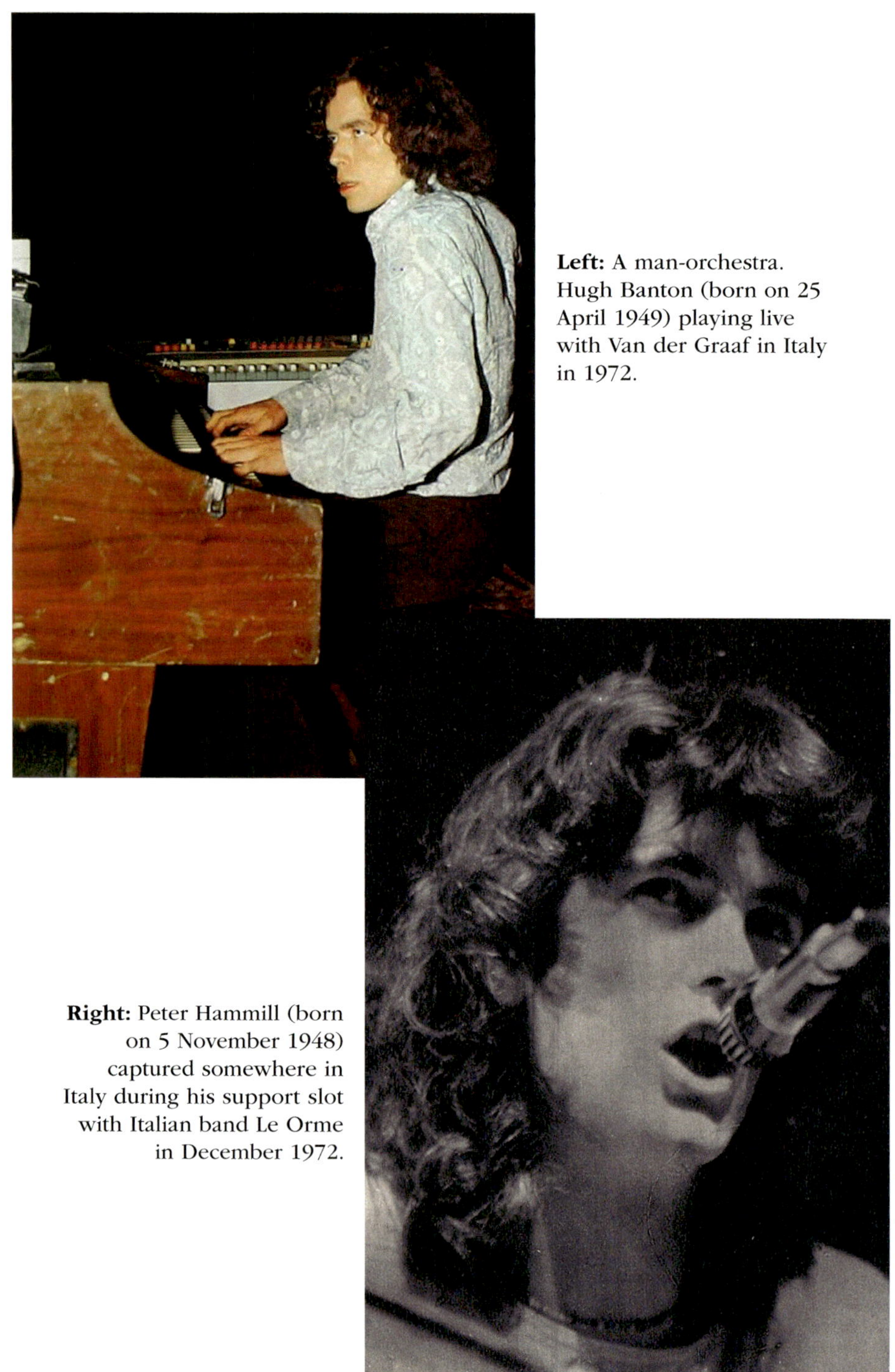

**Left:** A man-orchestra. Hugh Banton (born on 25 April 1949) playing live with Van der Graaf in Italy in 1972.

**Right:** Peter Hammill (born on 5 November 1948) captured somewhere in Italy during his support slot with Italian band Le Orme in December 1972.

**Right:** The electrified sax-machine. David Jackson (born on 15 April 1947) during a 1972 Van der Graaf show in Italy.

**Left:** The three-piece Van der Graaf lineup on stage in Trieste on 2 August 2009. *(Emilio Maestri)*

**Left (front) and below (back):** The first *Pawn Hearts* pressing used The Famous Charisma 'pink scroll' labels, as collectors call them, although their background colour is magenta to be more precise. The album track list was only displayed on labels, not on the cover. (*Charisma*)

**Below:** A psychedelic trip. The *Pawn Hearts* inner-sleeve photo, shot by Keith Morris. *(Charisma)*

(RIFF SECTION)
Yes, I know it's
Out of control, out of control:
(ACOUSTIC SECTION)
Greasy machinery slides on the rails,
Young minds and bodies on steel spokes impaled.
(RIFF SECTION)
Cogs tearing bones, cogs tearing bones;
(ACOUSTIC SECTION)
Iron-throated monsters are forcing the screams,
Mind and machinery box-press the dreams.

Particularly interesting is the sonic landscape of the two acoustic sections, where it's possible to identify the hiss of the wind in the distance/whizzes that sound similar to bird calls. Odriozola explains that all of this is produced by Banton's organ, in which a heavily distorted sound is filtered through a Wem tape delay. The 'whizz' is generated by the tape sliding against the heads of the device as the machine's motor is being switched on. A similar effect may be obtained by sliding the fingers along the fretboard of an amplified acoustic or electric guitar.

At this point, as the 'clockwork' set by man seems to be destined to continue its relentless run towards destruction, we come to a sudden turnaround (6.31).

But there still is time...

As these words are uttered, the four musicians launch into 40 seconds of complete improvisation, characterised by Banton's disconnected piano notes and the pounding beat of the drums. At its heart, it's a very jazzy improvisation, possibly the single moment when VdGG came closest to the jazz world in all their recordings. On the left channel, it's still possible to hear Hammill's acoustic guitar trying to cut through the sonic magma spilt out by the organ and the saxophone. However, it is the saxophone that calls the band 'to order' (7.10) by throwing in the main riff again but playing it in equal note values in 12/8. After that, the other instruments gradually follow suit, creating a triumphant reprise. There are more surprises to come, though: what was previously the 'theme' of the lemmings is now accepted by the protagonist but used instead to convey his intention to carry on living and fighting, over embracing their self-destructive nature:

Cowards are they who run today, the fight is beginning...
no war with knives, fight with our lives, lemmings can teach nothing;
Death offers no hope, we must grope for the unknown answer,
Unite our blood, abate the flood,
Avert the disaster.
There's other ways than screaming in the mob:

That makes us merely cogs of hatred.
Look to the why and where we are,
Look to yourselves and the stars, yes, and in the end
What choice is there left but to live
In the hope of saving
Our children's children's little ones?

The final part of the song (9.19 – 11.39) once again shows the band's high level of confidence in their musical skills and their ability to 'listen' to each other and interact, even in a recording studio situation. The tone becomes surprisingly subdued and sparse, rather similar, in a way, to that of another song recorded around the same time: the B-side 'W'. The 2021 Stephen W Tayler remixed version of the track revealed a new and beautiful musical detail that was cut off from the original version: at 11.15, a vibraphone enters the scene, adding an unexpected flavour to the coda.

Anyway, we can't tell if the main character is destined to succeed in his choices. In this regard, the sudden stop that closes the first track of the album almost seems to evoke the protagonist's leap of faith. The melancholy instrumental coda, vaguely reminiscent of the long improvised section from 'Moonchild' by King Crimson, closes the song with a touch of sadness and uncertainty, almost a painful resignation, as later stated by Hammill in his notes, published in the book *Killers, Angels, Refugees*:

> A song of extreme political ambivalence: at the time of writing, I was aware of both feelings and intended direction, but I now become more and more unsure; this, as the song, has to do with means rather than end, of which I have a degree of certainty. I have now arrived at a position in which I cannot decide whose voice is whose in the lyrics and can no more conclude whether the life-and-death style of the Lemmings in this context is desirable, good or bad than be sure that these abstractions have meaning in the overall life-line. The only conclusion which stands the test of time is that tending towards a far future hope, perhaps hope for a self-identification to replace my current ambiguous stance.

### **'Man-Erg'** (10.22)

After the hazy and undefined atmosphere of the 'Lemmings' coda, 'Man-Erg' opens in a rather clear and well-defined fashion: the descending chord progression played in 4/4 on the piano (F-E-D-C, with the higher octave C being played in all four chords as a harmonic tone) is easily identifiable and seems to be conveying quietude and peace of mind.

The piano Hammill is playing is the famous Trident Bechstein piano. It was there from the very early days of Trident: it was played on The Beatles' 'Hey Jude' in 1968 and featured on classic recordings by artists such as Paul McCartney, Rick Wakeman, David Bowie ('Life On Mars?'), Mick Ronson, Nicky Hopkins, Elton John ('Your Song'), Queen ('Bohemian Rhapsody'), Supertramp ('Crime Of The Century'). The piano is said to be difficult to play due to its stiff action; the hardened hammers give the piano a brighter and more powerful sound.

Lyrics-wise, *Pawn Hearts*' second track deals again with human nature and, more specifically, the different personalities that can coexist in a single person. This theme was quite dear to Hammill and would be tackled again in songs such as 'The Undercover Man', 'Mirror Images' and 'Lunatic In Knots'. In *Pilgrims #9*, Dean Carter calls 'Man-Erg' a 'no less than a painfully honest and stately hymn to the human situation, divided as we are between light and dark, between killer and angel.'

As Marco Olivotto explains in *Dark Figures Running*, the title of the song has a well-defined meaning:

> The title is a wordplay. 'Man' stands for man, while 'erg' is the unit of energy in the CGS system. It's an obsolete unit, corresponding to $10^{-7}$ Joules. 'Erg' has become a suffix generally indicating something concerning energy. Hammill's very own recommendation is to see 'man-erg' as you would 'horse-power', a unit of measurement of power. The best logical translation would simply be 'man-energy'.

Quite suggestive and somehow appropriate, although definitely not of chief importance, is the interpretation of 'erg' in its meaning of dune, a 'broad area of desert covered with wind-blown sand', which would fit nicely with the theme of the instability of human nature the song deals with: the protagonist of the song is unable to define his own attitude in a univocal way, shifting between different characters just like desert sand constantly changes its shape due to the blowing wind. Olivotto also points out how 'man erg' is actually an anagram for 'German', ideally echoing the notorious German tour, which, as seen previously, deeply influenced the lyrical and musical content of *Pawn Hearts*.

The opening verse of 'Man-Erg' begins:

> The killer lives inside me; yes, I can feel him move.
> Sometimes he's lightly sleeping in the quiet of his room,
> But then his eyes will rise and stare through mine,
> He'll speak my words and slice my mind inside.
> Yes, the killer lives.

It's impossible not to notice the link between the first words of the lyric and the almost identically titled novel by Jim Thompson – *The Killer Inside Me* (1952) – in which an unassuming, small Texas town cop conceals a sadistic, murderous nature, displaying a split personality. The 'room' is obviously the protagonist's mind, crowded by evil forces who sometimes take over, 'staring through' his eyes from the 'inside', as Hammill declares, thus determining his actions. The second verse further analyses the dichotomy inside the character:

The angels live inside me, I can feel them smile;
Their presence strokes and soothes the tempest in my mind
And their love can heal the wounds that I have wrought.
They watch me as I go to fall;
Well, I know I shall be caught
While the angels live.

This part, which is reprised almost identically at the end of the song, concludes the first section and leads to the well-known sax break (2.50). The following riff in 11/8 is repeated for no less than 32 bars by the electric piano (left channel) and distorted organ (right channel), with the sax playing either counterpoint or in unison. In bar ten of the riff (3.22), Hammill screams out:

How can I be free?
How can I get help?
Am I really me?
Am I someone else?

At 3.54, an impressive 'machine-like' ritardando starts, which painfully stretches the riff for another ten bars, sinking and coming to a halt on the third beat of the last riff bar. With the conclusion of the 32-bar riff, we arrive at a new section of the piece (4.30) in a much calmer environment. This section, which is three minutes in length, is also the longest segment in the whole song. Its 12/8 rhythm, divided in triplets, conjures up an oscillating effect that almost seems to cradle the listener. The sound of the electric piano becomes mellower, in contrast with the acid tones heard previously, and even the singing becomes more introspective:

But stalking in my cloisters hang the acolytes of gloom
And Death's Head throws his cloak into the corner of my room
And I am doomed.
But laughing in my courtyard play the pranksters of my youth
And solemn, waiting Old Man in the gables of the roof:
He tells me truth.

As Olivotto rightly points out in his notes, Hammill employs a spatial metaphor to associate the description of the state of his mind with the position of a number of subjects inside a hypothetical building. The courtyard hosts childhood memories – therefore, the past; the main room is crowded with the characters that presently throng his own mind; whilst close to the roof, in a higher position, he awaits the Old Man, who represents his future awareness.

Climaxing with David Jackson's wonderful sax solo, this section also features Robert Fripp on guitar: King Crimson's leader initially takes a secondary role, just playing accompaniment, only to gradually surface later during the sax part. For almost one minute (6.30 – 7.10), Fripp simply repeats an A note in different rhythmic patterns, in or out of time, finally merging together with the saxophone at 6.55, a unison which probably represents the emotional apex of the whole song.

As the instrumental portion comes to an end, Hammill feels the urge to go back to the opening section of the song, tying it somehow to the sax solo. Once again, it is Banton's hands, as seen previously during the analysis of the gestation of 'A Plague Of Lighthouse Keepers', which lead the band through a harmonic modulation from D Major to F Major, which will be further expanded towards the end of the piece.

Before that, however, the resumption of the singing sort of completes the parable of the main character:

> And I, too, live inside me and very often don't know who I am;
> I know I'm not a hero; well I hope that I'm not damned.
> I'm just a man, and killers, angels, all are these,
> Dictators, saviours, refugees in war and peace
> As long as Man lives...
>
> I'm just a man, and killers, angels, all are these:
> Dictators, saviours, refugees.

The initial dichotomy, represented by the killer and the angel (two entities in plain opposition), is not ultimately overcome: despite regaining some self-consciousness ('I, too, live inside me'), the protagonist continues to call out his fragmented nature, and even better, he projects it onto other figures (dictators, saviours, refugees) in an ideal gallery of characters destined somehow to coexist on earth. In reality, as Olivotto again correctly states, the solution is, in his words, to accept that 'I'm just a man', or rather, human nature is a source of uncertainty and he recognises the impossibility of self-definition. The leading figure's schizophrenia gets amplified by the partially dissonant sonic raids of a second piano (played by Banton) and the sax. This is then further highlighted by the overlapping of the 11/8 riff with the 6/4 harmonic progression from earlier. From 9.19 to 9.32, the band seem to be split in two: the voice (or better, the voices) and drums play the 11/8 riff against the piano, organ and sax playing the 6/4 progression.

The closing of the song is characterised by the same modular manoeuvre already used after the sax solo: the sounds become majestic and symphonic, with Evans overdubbing orchestral timpani. The ending of 'Man-Erg' is thus completely different from 'Lemmings', leaving no room for doubt, as Hammill made clear in *Killers, Angels, Refugees*: 'Index, appendix and clarification; it has all the positives that 'Lemmings' lacks.'

Renowned music journalist Sid Smith had this to say about 'Man-Erg' in a November 2022 online article for *Prog*: 'Impressive in both its sonic detail and actual performance, for many fans, the second track on *Pawn Hearts* represents everything that makes Van der Graaf Generator so special and beloved.'

## **Side B** (23.13)

### **'A Plague Of Lighthouse Keepers'** (23.13)

Here it is, taking the whole of side B, the complex multi-part suite that wreaked so much havoc within the band before its completion. Unsurprisingly, the analysis proves to be challenging right from the title: in English, the word 'plague' stands for 'an epidemic disease', and in its 'plague of' form (followed by a noun), it is closely associated with animal phenomena and destructive swarms of pests, like the giant hornets that invaded certain regions of China – 'a plague of hornets' – or the 'plague of spiders', sparked off by severe floods in Australia. 'Plague' is also the term used in the Bible for the ten calamities of Egypt, including 'the plague of locusts'. Therefore, the title of the suite refers to the unusual and mischievous proliferation of lighthouse keepers on planet Earth, an image somewhat presented on the album art as well, where the silhouettes of the pawns – inside which are portrayed various characters – ideally evoke many lighthouses scattered throughout the globe.

But who is the lighthouse keeper? Usually, it's an individual who not only lives in a state of forced isolation but owes this isolation to the fact that his dwelling is situated by the edge of the sea. The lighthouse keeper lives at the mercy of the sea and suffers its violence. While not physically affected by it – as the lighthouse is built to endure the power of the waves – his distress is essentially psychological. In the opening segment of the suite, 'Eyewitness', he's a privileged spectator of whatever occurs on the waters due to his high vantage point. The lighthouse keeper powerlessly watches people dying offshore, though his job must go on and the light must be kept lit. In *A Musical Guide To Pawn Hearts,* Ricardo Odriozola explains further:

> The existence of the lighthouse keeper is, first and foremost, a very lonely one. He works in a tower that emits light but is not receptive to it. Except for this light source, the tower is devoid of windows, making it an unlikely abode. The lighthouse keeper is witness to all that happens in the sea in front of him but is powerless to do anything about it other than keeping the light of the tower fed with the paraffin in the hope that it may serve as guidance to passing ships.

Odriozola points out how, of all times of the day, Hammill's focus falls on the night shift – that part of the work routine that takes place during the night when the keeper is required to sit next to the lantern to make sure the light works properly. Before him, only the endlessness of the sea. It's with this premise that the phenomenon of personalities spacing out/overlapping, as introduced in 'Man-Erg', takes place: '(A Plague) is a cinematic presentation of 'self' in several possible matrices', said Hammill in *Killers, Angels, Refugees*.

'Eyewitness' opens with a chord played on the Hohner electric piano by Hammill, a D minor to which a series of other notes are added.

Such dense harmony is altered by the built-in vibrato effect and a delay added in the mix that makes the repeating echoes sway from right to left. This chord, placed on the upbeat of the bar and the continuous ricocheting of notes that comes from it, seems to capture the sound of the waves crashing against the rocks. Odriozola mentions that even the vocal melody line is shaped in an arc form, giving the listener the impression of being rocked by the sea. Lyrics-wise, the text can be split into five different parts according to the type of singing Hammill employs:

(SINGLE FILTERED VOICE)
Still waiting for my saviour, storms tear me limb from limb;
My fingers feel like seaweed ... I'm so far out I'm too far in.

(SINGLE DRY VOICE)
I am a lonely man, my solitude is true,
My eyes have borne stark witness
And now my nights are numbered, too.

I've seen the smiles on dead hands,
The stars shine, but they're not for me.

(SINGLE FILTERED VOICE)
I prophesy disaster and then I count the cost...
I shine but, shining, dying, I know that I am almost lost.

(DISSONANT VOICES)
On the table lies blank paper and my tower is built on stone;
I only have blunt scissors, I only have the bluntest home.

(SINGLE FILTERED VOICE)
I've been the witness and the seal of death
Lingers in the molten wax that is my head.

While commenting on Dean Carter's analysis of the song (published in the fanzine *Pilgrims*), Sybilla Poortman, an avid reader of the fanzine, notes how Hammill's decision to employ different vocal timbres for different sections of the text couldn't possibly be a merely aesthetical choice. It's likely a way to give the different characters that crowd the lighthouse keeper's mind both a voice and a substance. The sections sung in an effect-filtered voice may as well be sung by the lighthouse itself or, to be precise, by the keeper identifying himself with the lighthouse.

In his annotated translation, Olivotto brings up the fact that the 'lighthouse-like' persona of the keeper seems to be obsessed and almost resigned to the idea of not being able to endure the strength of the sea, only to then be condemned to collapse under the wrath of yet another storm. Edgar Allan Poe's unfinished tale 'The Lighthouse' shares the same theme. In the story, written in diary form, the narrator arrives at the lighthouse and immediately explores its foundations to make sure the structure is sturdy. The connection between Hammill and Poe runs deep and became apparent a few years later when Hammill started working on the opera *The Fall Of The House Of Usher*, based on the short story of the same name by Poe. In the tale, one of the characters – Roderick Usher – develops a sort of symbiotic relationship with the old house he lives in, a house which he never manages to leave.

A small bit of trivia: the lyric 'I'm so far out I'm too far in' from 'Eyewitness' was quoted in the song 'Lord Of The Backstage' by Marillion on their 1985 concept album *Misplaced Childhood*. This is not a coincidence as Derek William Dick, better known as Fish, singer and lyricist of the band until 1989, has always been a big fan of Hammill's work.

The instrumental break that follows, titled 'Pictures Lighthouse', is actually divided into two parts. The first part is a musical representation of what was foreshadowed earlier ('I prophesy disaster and then I count the cost'). Jackson's horns magnificently recreate the sound of the sirens of two different ships in the mist, gradually approaching each other until the inevitable, catastrophic collision (3.50), mimed by the drums.

The second part, dominated by Banton's organ, is instead the musical transcription of the lighthouse keeper's state of mind after helplessly witnessing the wreck. This 'cinematic' relationship between music and events is emphasised in *Killers, Angels, Refugees* by a number of words annotated in brackets by Hammill next to this section:

(Eddies/rocks/ships/collision/remorse)

As Hammill explained to Olivotto, the five words represent a 'score of the instrumental passage, that also existed in the form of sketches' provided by Hammill to the rest of the band. The segment coming in after the crash, composed and played by Banton in real-time, is particularly beautiful, as he explained in *A Musical Guide To Pawn Hearts:*

As a matter of fact, it was take one! I certainly had pre-devised the style (Messiaen-type meandering!). We'd simply set up a tape echo on the organ and I went down to try it with the track (fast worker)...

**Pictures Lighthouse tracks list (Take 1)**

| | | |
|---|---|---|
| 1 | — | |
| 2 | — | |
| 3 | Drums | |
| 4 | Guide Vocal | |
| 5 | Sea Organ | Stereo |
| 6 | Sea Organ | Stereo |
| 7 | Organ II | Stereo |
| 8 | Organ II | Stereo |
| 9 | Seagulls Sax | |
| 10 | Seagulls Flute | |
| 11 | Ship I Sax | |
| 12 | Ship I Sax | |
| 13 | Ship II Sax | |
| 14 | Ship II Sax | |
| 15 | Organ | |
| 16 | — | |

Banton's improvisational piece runs its course as the second part of 'Eyewitness' starts (5.32), slowly fading away like a dream or a vision as reality comes to pass. Now, the lighthouse keeper faces his resignation and begins his voyage through the meanderings of his mind:

I am much too tired to speak
And as the waves crash on the bleak

Stones of the tower I start to freak
And find that I am overcome...

From this point on ('S. H. M.' – 6.47), the influence of Poe and Samuel Taylor Coleridge gets the better of Hammill's writing with the advent of various supernatural presences:

'Unreal, unreal' ghost helmsmen scream and fall in through the sky,
Not breaking through my seagull shrieks – no breaks until I die.
The spectres scratch on window slits,
The hollowed faces and mindless grins
Are only intent on destroying what they've lost.

The title of the track is the abbreviation of 'simple harmonic motion', which is defined as 'a special type of periodic motion an object experiences by means of a restoring force whose magnitude is directly proportional to the distance of the object from an equilibrium position and acts towards the equilibrium position. It results in an oscillation that is described by a sinusoid, which continues indefinitely'. The 'S.H.M.' title perhaps relates to the endless movement of the waves crashing towards the lighthouse, as exemplified by the 6/8 rhythm adopted in this section. Musically, this fourth part of the suite seems to gather momentum as a powerful fanfare-like idea, led by Jackson's tenor saxophone, is introduced, heavily contrasting with the scary encounters depicted in the lyrics. At the end of this section, when one of the lighthouse keeper's greatest fears – running out of fuel for his lamp – becomes apparent ('no paraffin for the flame'), the protagonist becomes taunted by the spectres gathered around him and gets overwhelmed by his own solitude ('Presence Of The Night' – 8.30):

'Alone, alone' the ghosts all call,
Pinpoint me in the light.
The only life I feel at all
Is the presence of the night.

Musically, 'Presence Of The Night' is built on a simple motif played by Hammill on the electric piano, around which the other instruments are invited to dance: Hugh Banton is on electric bass, while Robert Fripp makes another appearance on guitar. Dynamics-wise, this is also the part where the band touch the lowest end of the spectrum: at 10.34, Hammill's lone, spectral voice whispers the words 'Would you cry if I died?', only to reach the opposite end just a few minutes later. The overall stillness is indeed broken off by the movement that gradually leads to the instrumental maelstrom of 'Kosmos Tours', a reference to the German transport company from which Charisma rented the minuscule van used by Van der Graaf, Audience and Jackson Heights to travel around Germany in May 1971. The tight piano riff (12.14), composed and played by

Guy Evans, gets progressively reiterated by the other instruments, building up to a chaotic and inorganic series of almost endless refractions:

'That's me playing piano. I had to teach it to Hugh because it's not played with a conventional piano technique at all', said Guy Evans in *The Book*.
In this passage, the use of an ARP synthesiser, played by Banton, is of particular interest, as it wasn't an instrument commonly featured on other Van der Graaf Generator records. Hugh Banton talked about this in a *Private Conversation* piece from September 2013:

> The ARP synthesiser on *Pawn Hearts* (a 2500) belonged to Trident Studios, so that's why it wasn't a Moog. It was a big machine and the very latest technology, of course. Therefore, many bands wanted to use it when recording at Trident that year. (I'm pretty sure Peter used it subsequently on *Chameleon*). I think we mainly used it in the 'Kosmos Tours' section – Guy's riff – but there might be other minor appearances. I also used it at the end of 'Theme One', by the way. As I recall, the only other VdGG synth appearance is on *World Record* ... that was an ARP 2600.

On 'Kosmos Tours', the band decided to record in monaural 16 songs of their repertoire, one for each track available on the recording machine, with the intention of having them played all at once, thus creating a brief moment of total cacophony. The recording is only used for a few seconds right before the vocal entry at 13.17:

> The maelstrom of my memory
> Is a vampire and it feeds on me;
> Now, staggering madly, over the brink I fall.

'(Custard's) Last Stand' (13.35), composed by David Jackson, signals a return to peace and marks the character's moment of contemplation. The title is clearly a play on words between the name George Custer (the famed American colonel) and the dessert sauce.

> Lighthouses might house the key but can I reach the door?
>
> I want to walk on the sea so that I may better find a shore;
> But how can I ever keep my feet dry?
> I scan the horizon
> I must keep my eyes on all parts of me.

Looking back on the years it seems that I have lost my way:
Like a dog in the night, I have run to a manger,
Now I am the stranger I stay in.
Ah, well.

All of the grief I have seen leaves me chasing solitary peace;
But I hold experience in my head.
I'm too close to the light,
I don't think I see right, for I blind me.

As stressed by Olivotto, the lyrics to this section return to the area of investigation that was pivotal in 'Man-Erg': 'the multiple division of the 'self'' and the possibility to penetrate its true nature. The all-important mention of the door in the first verse, as seen in 'House With No Door' from *H To He* (1970), was later used by Hammill in an even more manifest way on 'Door', an unreleased song available on the double live album *Vital* (1978), where once more, the door represents the portal that grants access to one's 'I':

They're a blind man crouching by the pavement,
Only seeing with his third eye,
And clutching at the astral shadow
Of the door of a room
Called 'I'.

On top of that, the eyes of the hero must be kept 'on all parts of him', proof of the fragmentation of his personality that makes him a stranger to himself: hence a final act, blinding himself, as if it were from the outside, as though the deed were done by someone else. That is when the focus character's internal contradiction emerges more clearly and his quest for peace and isolation, his 'becoming lighthouse' to leave behind all the suffering he endured, turns him instead into a 'keeper of his own lighthouse', safe from his own tragedies while condemned to witness other people's misfortunes.

It's no coincidence that the following section, 'The Clot Thickens' (16.36), violently bursts the deceptive calm of '(Custard's) Last Stand' by re-establishing the old and familiar existential dilemmas:

Where is the God that guides my hand?
How can the hands of others reach me?
When will I find what I grope for?
Who is going to teach me?

The protagonist's awareness/dread of living with multiple personalities is once again palpable:

I am me/me are we/we can't see
Any way out of here.

However, it's the final words of this section, a direct reference to the two tracks on the first side, 'Lemmings' and 'Man-Erg' ('I'm just a man, and killers, angels, all are these'), that create a petrifying mental loop that seemingly puts the protagonist up against the wall:

I can see the lemmings coming, but I know I'm just a man.
Do I join or do I founder? Which can is the best I may?

As emphasised by Olivotto:

> It's quite peculiar that the suicide-prone lemmings are here seen in an apparently positive light: 'Do I join or do I founder?' ponders Hammill, as if joining the lemmings were a reasonable option. As a matter of fact, the question might as well be futile: the lemmings are eventually doomed to founder, fate is one and one only and the message conveyed is that there seems to be no 'better alternative.'

The true alternative, by contrast, could be expressed by the adversative conjunction 'but' in the first part of the sentence: the main character sees the lemmings coming *en masse* and knows their pernicious message, but once again, doesn't trust his own strength and resistance ('I know I'm just a man'). That's the foundation of his rhetorical question.

Musically, the piece is akin to a military march, a sort of sleazy, degenerate can-can that alternates between the 5/4, 6/4 and 5/8 time signatures, at the end of which (17.37) Hammill and the band engage in a call and response duel that escalates in the 7/8 riff played by the piano that characterises the remainder of the section. Odriozola explained further in *A Musical Guide To Pawn Hearts*:

> What remains of 'The Clot Thickens' is a turbulent seascape, only this time it is not being observed from a distance, as in 'Picture Lighthouse'. Our lighthouse keeper is now in the water, fighting, it would seem, for dear life. This is, in truly filmic fashion, drowning music.

Oddly enough, at 18.15, Hammill can be heard calling 'That's it, master', which was actually a cue for producer John Anthony, who was sitting at the mixing desk, to mute Hammill's microphone and stop the recording. Hammill's words ended up in the final mix by accident, but once the band realised the mistake, they decided to leave it on the record anyway. What's also worth mentioning is the presence of the Mellotron in this section. Although a very common and distinctive music instrument in the early 1970s, the Mellotron is only credited twice in the Van der Graaf Generator catalogue:

here on *Pawn Hearts* and five years later on *Still Life* (1976). As Dan Coffey correctly points out in his excellent book *Van der Graaf Generator On Track*: 'In sharp contrast to the Mellotron's usual role as a sombre, becalming agent in the realm of late 1960s/early 1970s progressive rock, Banton uses the instrument to project a sense of disorientation and unease, as though the chord were waves tossing the listener around on the sea.' Being a tape-based instrument, that peculiar effect is obtained by Banton operating on the tape speed control originally included on the instrument for tuning purposes. Also, as Stephen W. Tayler suggests, the tape machine speed itself could have been manipulated during the recording. The 1980 Charisma compilation *Repeat Performance* UK cassette (BGC 003) hosts an extended version of 'The Clot Thickens' as a bonus track, which is about 20 seconds longer than the *Pawn Hearts* version and features a different mix.

'Land's End (Sineline)/We Go Now', the final section of the suite, once again commences as the previous section halts abruptly, an indicator of the brutal editing together of pre-existing and partially self-contained compositions. These very last two, both penned by David Jackson, actually sparked the entire process of composition that led to the whole suite and its concept, as explained by David Jackson in *The Book*:

> I introduced that melody to Peter and talked to Hugh about it very early on. I wasn't sure how to arrange it, and Hugh said, 'Let's work on it.' Peter liked it very much and he wrote lyrics for it. Even though that song ended 'Lighthouse Keepers', we worked on it very early on, so that was the start.

The words that close 'A Plague Of Lighthouse Keepers' and, in essence, the whole chronicle of the lighthouse keeper – 'I think the end is the start' – might be another, perhaps coincidental, reference to this episode.

During the last four minutes of the suite, the musical component brightens up again, and just as in '(Custard's) Last Stand', the acoustic piano becomes the soundtrack to a further musing:

> Oceans drifting sideways, I am pulled into the spell,
> I feel you around me, I know you well.
> Stars slice horizons where the lines stand much too stark;
> I feel I am drowning – hands stretch in the dark.
>
> Camps of panoply and majesty, what is Freedom of Choice?
> Where do I stand in the pageantry, whose is my voice?
> It doesn't feel so very bad now, I think the end is the start,
> Begin to feel very glad now:
> All things are a part
> All things are apart
> All things are a part.

Thus, the saga ends … but how? According to David Jackson, 'Lighthouse Keepers' is simply the story of a lighthouse keeper who fails his duty and can't keep the tower's lamp lit. In reality, as Hammill explained to *Sounds* in 1972, it's up to the listener to decide the protagonist's fate:

> In the end ... well, it doesn't really have an end; it's really up to you to decide. He either kills himself, or he rationalises it all and can live in peace. Then, on a psychic/religious level, it's about him coming to terms with himself, and at the end, there's either him losing it all completely to insanity or transcendence; it's either way in the end. And then it's also about the individual coming to terms with society – that's the third level.

Towards the end, Hammill toys with the assonance between 'all things are a part' and 'all things are apart': all things are part of something unitary ('a part'), and at the same time, they are divided and alone ('apart'). Could this be the final revelation that strikes the lighthouse keeper at the end of his painful journey? Just as in David Lynch's films, the eventual interpretation might be much easier than it appears: everything in nature seems to be made of multiple parts destined to combine together to form a single thing. A book is made of pages and a musical piece is made of notes. Therefore, they are made of self-sufficient elements that can be coherently comprehended only in relationship to one another; all of them are essential for the completeness of the book or the musical piece. In much the same way, human nature and its psyche are composed of different shades and nuances that ultimately constitute the personality of the individual: fragmented (just think of the killers and angels in 'Man-Erg') yet simultaneously unitary, according to the way human nature is meant to be ('I'm just a man'). The problem is rather how to accept this reality, something that, perhaps, the lighthouse keeper eventually manages to do.

Musically, 'Lighthouse Keepers' closes with an instrumental section ('We Go Now') characterised by a great variety of timbres escalating through a solemn harmonic progression: the initial chord sequence of 'Land's End (Sineline)' gets reprised no less than five times in the final two minutes, but every repetition gets projected skywards in a vertical modulation that conveys an ascending vortex towards a peak that never really comes into sight. Odriozola points out that this is possibly due to the fact that the modulation spans a whole musical octave, and because of this, the chord progression appears to come back to where it started:

> Eb – F – G – A – B – C# – Eb

All of this has to be somehow tied to the urge, expressed in Hammill's writing, to pass on a feeling of incompleteness and uncertainty regarding the protagonist's fate, leaving him to his quest for answers to all the questions left unresolved. Regarding the ambiguous musical ending of the track, Dean Carter observed in *Pilgrims* #10: 'I can't describe the way these lads can end and yet not end a song. Best perhaps to say they invented the musical question mark.'

'We Go Now' concludes with the disturbing and persistent sound of the waves, only achieved through electrostatic synthesis, as if produced by Van der Graaf's gigantic generator emerging from the dark tides on the cover of *The Least We Can Do Is Wave To Each Other*. Back in 1972, in an article in the Italian magazine *Ciao 2001*, Maurizio Baiata defined the music of Van der Graaf Generator as 'music of the sea', referring to the lyrical content of tracks such as 'Killer' or 'Octopus' which, right from the title, clearly featured marine elements. As a matter of fact, the sea and other aquatic themes are prominent throughout all of Hammill and the Generator's early output, to the point of becoming almost paramount in 'A Plague Of Lighthouse Keepers'. Hammill delved deeper into this when interviewed by *Sounds* in 1972:

> Lyrically I have been into the sea for a long time – and not only lyrically; I have an incredible love/hate thing with the sea where it terrifies me, absolutely terrifies me, but it sucks at me as well – a horrible fascination.

## The World Is A Stage

> I still get asked who everyone is inside the floating pawns; some I remember, others I don't, but I still feel that it is the perfect piece of art for the record, the result of a very good collaborative working relationship with Peter. I also think that 'A Plague Of Lighthouse Keeper's is – without a doubt – the best piece of progressive music ever put on disc.
> Paul Whitehead

When the time arrived to create the artwork for *Pawn Hearts*, the band and Hammill, in particular, had no doubt about who to put in charge of the job: after all, Paul Whitehead had already created the artwork for the band's previous record, *H To He Who Am The Only One*, as well as the cover for the first Hammill solo album, *Fool's Mate*, released a few months earlier. Whitehead and the band met through producer John Anthony, who had already fostered a collaboration between the British artist and Genesis back when Paul was the artistic director of *Time Out In London* magazine. Founded in 1968 by Tony Elliott, the magazine was a weekly guide that detailed events and activities (live shows, exhibitions, film screenings, plays) and the best restaurants and live clubs in the city. On his website, Paul said:

> Naturally, every band – both the up-and-coming hopefuls and the already successful – came through our doors to place an ad or seek a review of their latest LP. My design skills were often called on and then I met Genesis through their producer.

Whitehead became an album artwork designer as early as 1967 when he took care of the re-packaging of some reissues for US label Liberty Records, who, in 1969, commissioned him to design the cover for High Tides' debut album, *Sea Shanties*. John Anthony suggested that Van der Graaf should consider a collaboration with Whitehead for the album *H To He Who Am The Only One* since the band weren't happy with the way that CCS Advertising had handled the artwork for the previous record, *The Least We Can Do Is Wave To Each Other*. When Hammill met Whitehead to talk about the graphics for *H To He*, the two immediately found themselves on the same wavelength, although the initial prototype was rejected and a previous painting from the artist was instead used as the final cover for the LP, as Whitehead outlined in *The Book*:

> I actually had a painting that I'd done earlier for myself. I'm a Libra and that was my interpretation of the birth of Libra. It was called 'Birthday'. The eye beam goes right down to London. I visualised my birth; that was me being born.

Besides its well-known cover, Whitehead also designed the inside illustration of the gatefold LP. In this case, the work was inspired by the lyrics to one of the songs on the record: opening the outer gatefold sleeve, one can indeed see the 'fingers groping for the galaxies' described by Hammill at the beginning of 'Pioneers Over C'. At the end of the day, one of the best things about Paul was that he could really grasp the musical universe and lyrical mythos of the bands he worked with, following the whole creative process in the studio and getting to know the musicians personally until he almost became part of the crew. In *The Book*, Whitehead went into more detail:

> When I created the cover for the first Hammill solo album, *Fool's Mate*, a lot of the stuff came up in the recording sessions. There were jokes that were made about something, stuff that was actually said or talked about or something that would crack everybody up in the middle of the sessions. It was very topical, like, 'Hey, I'll put that on the cover!' And they'd say, 'Yeah, great, put that on the cover!' ... Peter told me that fool's mate is the quickest way to finish a chess game. It's checkmate in three moves, so he gave me the board set up in Fool's Mate and that's how I painted it.

Whitehead began working on the artwork for *Pawn Hearts* after a briefing with Hammill and started to develop his ideas while attending the band's rehearsals. Their relationship was firm by now, and undoubtedly, the band were pleased that the artist would work on the artwork in their presence while being able to update them in real-time on the progress. Compared with the previous cover art, this time, Whitehead's creation was much more complex. The album art of *Pawn Hearts*, besides spreading on both the front and back cover, as it did on *Fool's Mate*, featured several different techniques, like gouache painting, collage and airbrush painting. In a 2013 *Private Conversation* piece, Whitehead explained the thinking behind the artwork:

> When I was assigned to VdGG to talk to them about doing this record cover, Peter Hammill was most adamant that he wanted 'something very different from my work with Genesis.' I was dabbling in airbrush artwork at the time and that seemed to be quite a contrast from the paintings I'd made for Genesis. The idea came from a talk Peter and I had about 'All the world's a stage' and how we are all pawns on that stage no matter who or what we are in life.

In order to visually represent these concepts, Whitehead came up with the idea of organising the background of the cover – which depicted a set of clouds – in such a way that it would bring to mind the image of a theatrical set or a stage curtain: this was probably inspired by the 1960 painting *Les Mémoires D'un Saint* by Magritte, where red/rust-coloured curtains open to reveal a blue sky and white clouds to the viewer. He then drew planet

Earth, over which he arranged a series of characters, some historical – like Napoleon or John Lennon – and others anonymous, placing them inside silhouettes of see-through pawns. To paint the characters, Whitehead took inspiration from the 'cigarette cards' that many tobacco manufacturers included in cigarette packets between the late 1800s and the 1940s: those small cards portrayed actors, actresses, baseball players or Indian chiefs. Quite cleverly, in England, the cards were issued in sets, usually made of 25 or 50 cards, featuring a common theme and were meant to be collected as a set. For example, there was a set depicting the most famous castles and abbeys in the UK, another set dedicated to the most beloved cricket players and so on. This made the cards a rather desirable object for collectors, and some of these items still fetch considerable prices at auctions. In the same *Private Conversation* piece, Whitehead detailed the key elements of the artwork:

> The background – the planet Earth and the theatrical curtain – were painted in gouache. The painting technique of gouache is a method in which a kind of tempera paint is made heavier and more opaque by the addition of a white pigment, such as chalk or white lead, then bound with gum arabic. This results in a paint that is more opaque and glossier than traditional tempera paint. The technique is still very much used to produce decals and theatrical backdrops. All the characters were drawn by me from English cigarette cards, coloured in gouache and then cut out and pasted onto the background. The chess pieces were airbrushed over the top on a sheet of clear acetate, and the title was cut out of speckled paper and pasted on the acetate layer. This was 'layers' way before Photoshop.

Using an array of different techniques, Whitehead managed to eternally bind the artwork not only to the title of the album, the 'pawn hearts', but also, as per Hammill's request, to the macro-theme that underlies the whole record: man is but a pawn in a scheme much bigger than he could fathom. Therefore, it doesn't matter if he's a pauper, a king or a killer because, ultimately, his actions will always be part of a master plan that he won't be able to comprehend. That automatically leads to the association of the characters with the pawn, as the pawn is the weakest piece and the one whose freedom of movement is most limited in the game of chess.

Over the years, the most common question asked of Whitehead concerns the various characters on the cover of *Pawn Hearts* and whether he could identify them as personalities that actually exist or existed. In 1997, the artist agreed to examine every pawn with Jim Christopulos in an interview that was partially issued in the fanzine *Pilgrims* initially before later being fully published on the website vandergraafgenerator.co.uk (see colour section for more detail).

Thanks to the idea of portraying the characters inside clear chess pieces, Whitehead succeeded in conveying another visual element that was central to the album: if one looks closely, the shape of a pawn and the shape of a lighthouse are pretty much alike. Hence, the cover features the visual manifestation of that 'plague of lighthouse keepers' from the eponymous song. Once completed, Whitehead's art piece was taken to Charisma's offices to be photographed and impressed on the printed sheet. The original dimensions of the painting were exactly those of the unfolded cover of the album. Unfortunately, Paul does not own the original artwork anymore. For the PH & VdGG Study Group's *Pawn Hearts* Day event in Guastalla in August 2007, Whitehead shared a message:

> The thing that I remember the most about *Pawn Hearts* is hearing it for the first time. It was in Trident Studios and I arrived just as they were finishing the first mix. It was done manually, so at least five pairs of hands were manipulating the sliders on the mixing desk in real-time. Then, someone rolled a very large funny cigarette (which was about six inches long and shaped like a cone). We all took a puff on it and John Anthony 'rolled tape'. To say that it was an extraordinary experience would be an understatement – especially as all of our senses were somewhat heightened – and I think that everyone in the room was impressed. I had only heard bits and pieces as I designed the artwork and I had never heard the whole piece. 'How will it play on Radio One?' someone asked and we all cracked up.

In October 1971, Charisma released *Pawn Hearts* in England in a classic gatefold cover (a cover that could be opened to reveal a full picture) as they had already done with *The Least We Can Do* and *H To He*. What awaits inside the package is so peculiar that it deserves a thorough clarification. The notorious picture portrays the four members in front of Tony Stratton Smith's country house in Crowborough, where the band used to rehearse. The picture was taken by rock photographer Keith Morris on infra-red film, which explains the surreal colours of the scene (the green leaves of the trees being shown in red is one example), but what really strikes the observer is the way the four musicians are captured: Banton, Hammill and Evans are standing up on a wooden table, whilst Jackson is right in front of them, holding a football under his arm. All four are wearing black shirts and they are performing the Nazi salute. In a 1972 letter to Jem Shotts, Hamill explained how it came about:

> So we took lots of shots of that (all of which are equally weird) and then had a few frames left, so we got into the psychedelic Nazi's trip! When we saw the effect, the pose, infra-red film and all, we instantly overcame any inhibitions about freaking people and knew it HAD to be that!

The picture today would cause its fair share of embarrassment, as the musicians later admitted, but as a matter of fact, it was the result of an intricate series of coincidences:

Firstly, there was Crowborough Tennis, a game the four had invented during rehearsals at Luxford House. The game was played by one participant (or two) standing up on a table while another player simply stood up on the ground in front of him at some distance. The player on the table would 'serve' the football by throwing it to bounce once on the table; then, the opponent would 'return' it so that the ball would bounce again on the table. Points were awarded if the ball touched the ground, if the ball didn't hit the table, if a player missed the ball or if it bounced twice on the table. In the picture on the inside of *Pawn Hearts*, one can see David Jackson holding a football under his arm (although often mistaken for a globe), and in front of him, his three bandmates are standing up on the table, as the photo shoot was meant to document a number of phases of this bizarre game.

Secondly, the black shirts (and the yellow ties) refer to the 'Blackshirts' society, as Hammill explains in various interviews. During the recording of the album, everybody went insane (including producer John Anthony and sound engineer Robin Cable), so they came up with the idea of forming a company and a society to unite all those who pushed the boundaries of sanity. That was what 'Blackshirts' society was about. Of course, it didn't have anything to do with politics; it was merely a surreal and exclusive coterie. During the photo session for the album, the idea resurfaced again and the band thought it funny enough to use it.

Finally, the Nazi salute is again a result of a series of criss-crossed circumstances. The so-called 'Psychedelic Nazi's Trip' was certainly instigated by the state of hyper-excitement the band were in during rehearsals, combined with the black shirts they wore. But there's more to it. The pose they struck was also a comical reference to a statue seen in Kaiserslautern during the renowned German tour in the spring of 1971, which portrayed some German soldiers giving the salute. Hugh Banton detailed this further in *The Book*:

> There was definitely both a Monty Python and a surrealist influence there. We were in uniform – black shirts and yellow ties – and apparently giving a Nazi salute. Black shirts were a 1940s British Nationalist party uniform – heavy right-wing bad stuff. The Pythons had regularly sent up Nazi Germany and, of course, 1971 was in the middle of the Python era. We'd been to Germany recently and figured Germany was ripe for ridicule at every opportunity. But it's all ultimately inexplicable and immensely politically incorrect – long before political correctness had been invented. You just wouldn't get away with this nowadays, but I think the unfathomability was the attraction! Like, how bizarre can we make this?

The credits were placed at the bottom-left of the picture, while the package didn't include the lyrics this time – a departure from the two previous records, which did contain them. In fact, each copy of the album was supposed to come with a lyric sheet, a black sheet of paper with text printed in white on one side only, embellished by a drawing of a pawn carrying a heart. The sheet was only included with a limited number of copies, making it a highly sought-after item for collectors.

In conclusion, it's rather funny to be reminded that the title of the album – quite appropriate given the content and the themes and definitely of pivotal importance to the cover concept – actually came from an unintentional play on words by David Jackson, outlined by Hugh Banton in *The Book*:

> Dave Jackson one time said: 'I'll go down to the studio and dub some more porn harts.' Of course, he meant to say 'horn parts', so that's the origin of that!

When I wrote my book *Van der Graaf Generator. Behind And Beyond - Le Storie Dietro Le Copertine,* I asked some of the band's fans and music critics to select their favourite Van der Graaf artwork. Sid Smith chose the *Pawn Hearts* album cover and told me the following story:

> I was familiar with the cover of *Pawn Hearts* for a long time before I heard the three pieces that made up the album. Sometime in late 1971 or early 1972, I first encountered the outside of the gatefold sleeve spread out and stapled to the wall of a record shop I used to go to whenever I could. This was a time when money was scarce, so these visits didn't usually result in any purchases. However, you could at least flick through the racks and soak up the atmosphere. Seeing planet Earth hovering on the cosmic stage with those archetypal figures in their transparent pawn casings, swirling in chaotic orbits, presented a grand and mysterious vista where all kinds of stories and connections surged before me, waiting to be explored and understood. Whatever the intentions or underlying concepts the artist may have had, on every visit to the shop, my teenage psyche was engaged on a mission to decode and decipher the assembly of historical and mythical figures, creating narratives forged by the vagaries of coincidence and chance cultural connections. It was a cover with a life of its own. Back then, the music still unheard, I tried to imagine what these songs would sound like. I knew they would be epic, bold, cryptic, majestic and, above all, adventurous. With a cover like this, how could they be anything else?

## Whatever Would Robert Have Said?

> Hammill said that when he began singing, he wanted to be the vocal equivalent of Hendrix. Conceptually, he was right on the beam. And he delivers, I think.
> Robert Fripp

Among all the topics surrounding *Pawn Hearts*, there's certainly one that deserves a whole chapter of its own: the prestigious guest, Robert Fripp. The magnitude of what Fripp had accomplished with King Crimson back in those days was astounding: one only needs to think how *In The Court Of The Crimson King* changed the course of music in 1969, paving the way for the progressive rock phenomenon of the 1970s. David Jackson recalled the power of *In The Court* during a Mick Dillingham interview in 1990:

> I remember hearing *In The Court Of The Crimson King* while I was in the band Heebalob and the music was unbelievable; it had the same impact as *Sgt Pepper* before it. The possibilities it opened, especially in the direction I was going, were amazing.

Before *Pawn Hearts*, Fripp had already teamed up with the band on their previous album, *H To He Who Am The Only One* (1970), for which he recorded two guitar tracks for the song 'The Emperor In His War Room'. The collaboration between Fripp and Van der Graaf stemmed from an explicit request from Hammill to producer John Anthony, outlined by Hammill in a 1971 *Melody Maker* interview:

> I didn't know Bob before the session, but I knew I wanted to use him because he plays pictures and that's what I think it's all about. It actually came about because I'd mentioned it to John Anthony, our producer, and he bumped into Bob one night and asked him to do it.

John Anthony detailed his communication with Fripp in *The Book*:

> I would see King Crimson around. They'd play at the Marquee and I always used to sit and chat with Fripp. Then, one day, I called him up and I said, 'Fripp, do you want to do a session?' He said, 'I've never done a session before.' I said, 'Come on, it's for Peter Hammill and Van der Graaf!'

Fripp was likely aware of Van der Graaf's output at that point. What's beyond doubt, though, is that the Manchester band held him in the highest regard, as exemplified by David Jackson in the same 1990 interview:

> There had been a feeling within the band that, for recording purposes, a guitar was needed at points. Hugh and I didn't feel this, but Guy certainly did.

> Nic (Potter) had done a bit of guitarring on *The Least We Can Do*, but the argument went out of the window when the chance came to have Fripp on the album! At that time, Fripp was seen as an innovator and it certainly gave us massive credibility having him on there.

Hammill's first solo album, *Fool's Mate*, recorded a few months after the sessions for *H To He*, again benefited from the presence of Crimson's leader, further proof of the mutual admiration that had been established by now between Fripp and the band. On this occasion, Fripp played guitar on five of the songs. Despite the reverence, though, Fripp's unorthodox working methods baffled the whole band, as outlined by John Anthony in *The Book*:

> At the time of recording *The Least We Can Do*, he showed up and didn't have a tape beforehand. He listened to it once all the way through and said, 'Right, I'll do two takes and keep whichever bits of whichever takes – no more.'

In the same 1990 interview, David Jackson has his own memories of Fripp:

> I can remember him coming down to Trident, setting all his pedals up and plugging his guitar in, putting his headphones on, although he'd never heard the track before. He recorded this amazing solo on 'The Emperor In His War Room' in the first take – and that first take was the best; he didn't improve on it. He actually ended up rejecting it. There were a couple of off notes because he didn't know where the track was going at points, but there was a spirit about that first take that was supreme and we were all awestruck.

In contrast to *H To He* and *Fool's Mate* credits, where Fripp is clearly acknowledged for the songs where he does appear, in *Pawn Hearts*, there's no specification as to what tracks he actually plays on. This led many critics and fans to misinterpret guitar tracks as other instruments, such as the organ and the saxophone, filtered through a myriad of pedals and effects. For example, as noted by Odriozola in his manuscript, the distorted sound that counterpoints Hammill's vocal part and then bleeds into the coda of 'A Plague Of Lighthouse Keepers' during the track's majestic finale isn't Fripp's guitar but rather a fuzz box-warped organ played by Banton.

Thanks to the info provided by Stephen W Tayler, who remixed the whole album for the *Charisma Years* 2021 box set, we can now almost certainly be sure of Fripp's specific appearances on the album:

### 'Lemmings'

According to Tayler, on the original multitrack tape, Robert Fripp's electric guitar take starts at around the six-minute mark on the right-hand side of the mix. He was recorded up until the end of the song, but it wasn't all used in the original version – only the menacing section from 6.40 to 7.17 was included. Unfortunately, while creating the new 5.1 and stereo mix of the album, Tayler decided to match what was used for the original mix, so the full Fripp track was not revealed. Anyway, Tayler confirmed that the brief and strange noise at 9.50 on the original mix (right-hand side) that sounds a bit like a cello is actually a tiny part of Fripp's guitar track.

**'Man-Erg'**

Fripp gets involved only in the central section of the song, from 4.41 to 7.10. The interplay between the guitar and the saxophone that culminates at 6.51 is of rare beauty. With careful listening, it's possible to notice Fripp playing just one note continuously, a similar technique employed during the instrumental break of King Crimson's 'Starless' in 1974, where the guitar keeps repeating the same figure on one note, ascending the note for every chord change. On 'Man-Erg', Fripp obsessively repeats the same A note for almost one minute, altering both volume and rhythm until his note fuses with the A played by the saxophone at the peak of its solo.

**'A Plague Of Lighthouse Keepers'**

Fripp plays a very delicate, albeit clearly audible, guitar part in the section titled 'Presence Of The Night', starting from 8.30. According to the original track sheet for the album, an electric guitar track was also recorded on both parts of 'Eyewitness' but was not included on either the 1971 or 2021 mix.

After *Pawn Hearts*, Fripp's and Van der Graaf Generator's artistic paths wouldn't cross again. Fripp and Hammill would, however, still keep in touch and Fripp would ask the Generator's leader to sing on his 1979 solo album *Exposure*. There were reports of fans spotting Fripp in the crowd during Hammill's US solo tour in February 1978, but the most amusing moment of their saga occurred when Van der Graaf played their legendary New York concert on 18 October 1976 at the Beacon Theatre. When the rumours of Fripp being in the audience began to spread, the crowd went mental and started chanting, 'Bring out Fripp, bring out Fripp', hoping that the guitarist would get on stage for an impromptu session. Hammill, from the stage, smiled and quietly replied: 'Well, Fripp has been trying to bring out Fripp for years, and every time, it's a bloody disaster!

## A Chink In The Curtain

> I have to confess complete ignorance of precisely what Van der Graaf Generator are trying to achieve. Really.
> A review of *Pawn Hearts* by *Record Mirror* in December 1971

### October 1971

*Pawn Hearts* was released by the Charisma label in October 1971. Oddly enough, most of the albums that the band made would be released between September and December. After the release of their fourth album, the band felt that they had reached their top in terms of expression and were deeply excited to have been able to complete such a complex track as 'A Plague Of Lighthouse Keepers'.

Unfortunately, the recognition that Van der Graaf Generator were aiming for would not be achieved for many years. The reaction of the English press to *Pawn Hearts* was actually contrasting. On one side, Roy Hollingworth in *Melody Maker,* dated 6 November 1971, shared a positive reaction ("A Plague Of Lighthouse Keepers', the mammoth eight-part poetical and musical saga on the new Van der Graaf album *Pawn Hearts*, is one of the most fascinating and dramatic items I've ever heard') but other musical reviewers had a different opinion: 'To me, the album was something of a disappointment because I felt they'd stretched themselves too far along the way they'd been going, and instead of a chilling, disturbing but completely believable album, had tipped over into incredible melodrama' (*Sounds*, 29 January 1972). In December 1971, *Record Mirror*, while acknowledging the band's talent, took a similar view:

> Their music is forever verging on the hysterical and I suppose if you should have a particular penchant for the unbalanced, then this is the vinyl platter you've been waiting for kids. As musicians, they are certainly more than competent. Flurries of time changes, weird voicings and intricate arrangements, especially on side two's 'A Plague Of Lighthouse Keepers', a concept of sorts. But I do grow weary of endless meanderings and that, to me, is what *Pawn Hearts* ends up as.

Apart from the difference of opinions among the English reviewers, the point was that *Pawn Hearts*, just like the previous *H To He Who Am The Only One*, couldn't make it into the English hit parade. In fact, it had done even worse than the previous albums in terms of sales; it looked like *The Least We Can Do Is Wave To Each Other* was meant to be the only VdGG album to hit the English top 100. 'It was frustrating, but that's just the nature of the music. Van der Graaf were never going to be enormous. Just like classical music. It has a limited audience', said Hugh Banton in *The Book.*

The poor feedback on the sales of the new album had some influence on the band's relationship with the label. Charisma Records, who had already refused the band's idea of releasing *Pawn Hearts* in a double format, decided to concentrate all resources on other bands in their roster, such as Lindisfarne, who, at that time, were able to get to the top of the charts with the album *Fog On The Tyne*. Tony Stratton Smith's tactic to aid the band re-emerge from the quicksand they had sunk in was just the same: the four of them had to play as many gigs as possible to promote the new album. So, following the release of *Pawn Hearts*, they played about 50 gigs, most of them in small University venues, and mainly together with Genesis, who were also under contract with Charisma and in desperate need of commercial success. But even in a live setting, the band had to face the technical difficulties inherent in the material released and were forced to remove 'A Plague Of Lighthouse Keepers' – the most representative track on *Pawn Hearts* – from their setlists.

The band started to think about gaining some popularity through little media operations that would somehow highlight the surreal and ironic side of their music. It is probably for this reason that, when performing another BBC Session in December 1971, they decided to play 'Lemmings', 'Refugees' and an unreleased composition named 'An Epidemic Of Father Christmases'. The track, about five minutes long, had actually been composed by Hammill and Chris Judge Smith, another founder of the band, a few years earlier. It was a Christmas parody that opened with the 'Silent Night' choral theme before transitioning to the typical Christmas theme of 'Rudolph the Red-Nosed Reindeer'. After a quick hint of 'Man-Erg', guest vocalist Judge Smith begins singing in the role of Santa Claus. In the final coda, after a short mention of the themes of the 'Troika' from the *Lieutenant Kijé Suite* by Prokofiev and the overture of the *Carmen* by Bizet, the quintet wish a Merry Christmas to all listeners on the notes of 'We Wish You A Merry Christmas'. In *The Book*, Hugh Banton detailed the thinking behind this:

> I think we were just sort of making fun of ourselves, as usual. Everyone was taking 'A Plague Of Lighthouse Keepers' so seriously in terms of 'what does it mean?' and all that. So, we all thought that it was very funny to do it.

## January 1972

The promotion of the band by Charisma at the beginning of 1972 was more positive. In fact, in January, the band suddenly announced the release of a 45 rpm single that also included a remake of BBC Radio 1's morning opening theme. The new national broadcasting station, launched on 30 September 1967 as a replacement for the pirate radios that illegally transmitted from ships anchored in the English seas, had commissioned the theme to George Martin, the famous producer of The Beatles, who had conveniently titled it 'Theme One'. Certainly, following the issue of a work like *Pawn Hearts,* the idea of releasing the cover of a radio theme just a few months later was bizarre enough, as Hammill himself admitted in a

*Sounds* interview of that time, significantly titled 'Van der Graaf open a chink in the curtain':

> Though 'Theme One' is highly unrepresentative of the Van der Graaf we know, it's a part of what we do. And it's all part of Van der Graaf's post-*Pawn Hearts* idea of trying to reach more people by using parts of that whole, which is Van der Graaf Generator, which they haven't really drawn on before.

Since the time of the glorious *Six Bob Tour*, the band had enjoyed performing instrumental tracks – containing quotes and reworked versions of famous old songs of the 1960s, like 'Telstar' by Tornadoes or even TV themes, such as the *Star Trek* theme – as encores. In *The Book*, Guy Evans sang Banton's praises when it came to composing these tracks:

> The thing was that Hugh Banton could play anything, and he would just pull these things out of his hat. It was quite a nice antidote to the extremely dark and full-on Van der Graaf set that had preceded it.

In the case of 'Theme One', the idea of the three Generators creating a rock 'n' roll arrangement (the original theme was recorded by Martin with a whole orchestra and minimal rhythmic incidental music) originated directly from the daily experience of the band, as outlined by David Jackson in *Wonderous Stories* #16 in December 2009:

> 'Theme One' had an enormous sort of political significance in 1971 because you had pop music and that was broadcast on the light program, so the BBC had total control. There were no independent radio stations; it was all BBC and the BBC decided what we could listen to. So, pirate radio stations were born, but before that, there was Radio Luxembourg: all the young people used to listen to Luxembourg. I listened to Luxembourg when I was very young to listen to pop music, rock, blues and other stuff. Then, the pirates came and set up radio stations all around the country in boats, in ships, so the BBC realised: 'Hang on, we're losing all our audience, we've got to do something.' So, in 1971, they said, 'Let's completely change the BBC – let's create Radio 1', and they took the best DJs from the pirates and gave them jobs, gave them respectability. To seal these things, they said: 'We have a new program called Radio 1. We need a theme: who is the best composer? Who is the only person who can write such a theme? Well, of course, The Beatles man, George Martin! So, he wrote that fantastic tune and it was played at 6 o'clock every morning, at the start of Radio 1 programs, and at 6 o'clock most days, we were on the motorway driving home and I was always driving, so I was in control of the radio and the other guys were usually asleep. I love driving, driving very fast. So, at 6 o'clock, 'Theme One' is on the radio and they all wake up and we all sing it.

The real baptism of fire for the new version of 'Theme One' happened in an unexpected way during the well-known concerts in Germany in the spring of 1971. Once again, the notorious German tour served to heavily influence the production of the band, again outlined by David Jackson in an October 2013 *Private Conversation* piece:

> We must have rehearsed it, but I don't remember rehearsing it. At those particular times, we were doing very well and Peter was really the spokesman of the band and doing lots and lots of interviews. In early 1971, we made a very famous tour, the *Six Bob Tour*, and maybe we started playing that; I don't know exactly, but the most important event was in the spring in Munich. We were doing a very, very big event and Charisma Records were really on a push, trying to get European record companies involved in the whole Charisma Records and there was this very important event at the Circus in Munich. Peter wasn't available, but there were lots and lots of important people there. We were the headline act and were doing the soundcheck first. Someone told us, 'Please play something!!', and, of course, without Peter there, it's not so easy, so we played 'Theme One' and they were just like, 'WOW – play it again, that was great' – they loved it. So, the Company said, 'Right, next week, you're going to the studio to record it'; they were suddenly thinking that they'd got a hit because our previous single, 'Refugees', wasn't a hit.

According to Banton in *The Book*, it was Gail Colson, Charisma Label Manager at that time, who pushed the band to record a new version of 'Theme One', suggesting that they add it to their setlist to open their live gigs: 'You play 'Theme One', then comes Peter.' It seemed a good idea. Even Hammill, who hadn't taken part in the studio recordings, liked it. So, since that day, 'Theme One' was always played live, sometimes as the concert's closing theme, with Peter enjoying jumping from one side to the other of the stage, running up and down and climbing the PA system. In a 1972 personal letter to Jem Shotts, Hammill communicated his opinion of the song:

> 'Theme One' came about initially as a rehearsal knockabout by the others, being a groovy toon, and gradually became a part of our set. As there seemed no real place for it on an album, it was released as a single, as we felt it stood a chance of getting through to people not normally exposed to us, perhaps pulling a few of them round!! It could be regarded as a sell-out, a cop-out from our usual self, but then it's bad if you're always your usual self, but it is deadly to take yourself too seriously all the time. I guess the nature of your coming to hear it indicates some level of success. Incidentally, it's got f*** all to do with me apart from authorisation ... I wasn't even there when it was recorded!!

On 4 February 1972, 'Theme One' was finally released as a single in England. The Van der Graaf Generator version opened with the grandiose sound of a pipe organ that was recorded by Hugh Banton and John Anthony at the Saint Marylebone Paris Church of London, near Regent's Park. The organ is no longer in the Church and is now held by the Burtley Fen Collection in Pinchbeck, Lincolnshire. The B-side of the single contained an unreleased track, titled 'W', with mysterious and rarefied atmospheres, which were intentionally in contrast with the cheerful sound on the other side. Nevertheless, 'Theme One' was unable to bring Van der Graaf Generator into the charts, something that had not happened since the spring of 1970 when they had reached number 47 with *The Least We Can Do Is Wave To Each Other*. The single was also released in Italy on 15 February 1972, right after the first gigs in that country, then in Germany, France and even Australia. In the first three countries, the cover artwork was different from the English edition, which simply used the same photo of the band from the inner gatefold image of the *Pawn Hearts* album. The track became rather popular in Italy (reaching number 11 in the singles charts) and was also released in a jukebox version with 'A Hard Rain's Gonna Fall' by Leon Russell as a B-side. A few months later, Charisma took the opportunity to include 'Theme One' directly on the American release of *Pawn Hearts*, questionably placing the song on the first side of the album between 'Lemmings' and 'Man-Erg'. Obviously, Hammill did not appreciate it, as outlined in a KNAC Radio interview in 1978:

> I didn't know anything about it going on *Pawn Hearts* in the States until it happened. For me, *Pawn Hearts* is 'Lemmings', 'Man-Erg' and 'Lighthouse Keepers'. Putting 'Theme One' between 'Lemmings' and 'Man-Erg' breaks it up a bit. I mean, 'Lemmings' drifts out, and with 'Man-Erg', you get some sort of affirmation after seemingly all hope is gone. If, suddenly, you've got all hope gone and then there's a jolly tune going on in there, and *then* you've got affirmation, it's rather difficult!

Still, after many years, the main question stays the same: why did 'Theme One' not become a success in England in spite of its potential? David Jackson attempted to answer this during a *Private Conversation* interview in October 2013:

> If questions were asked, and I think they were, Charisma Records had a guy called 'the plugger'. A plugger was a guy who had boxes of singles and went knocking on people's doors saying: 'Play this'. And the man says, 'How much have you got?' and money then changes hands. So, you get the record, you get some money and then you play it. He has to persuade the DJs to play the record. I'm sure that happened; it had to happen because it's Radio 1

> now. We are not talking about pirates; no one could go around and find a pirate in a boat and give them the record ... they were all-powerful, and by the time they worked for the BBC, they were bloody gods and very powerful, probably with big salaries ... So why wasn't 'Theme One' doing airplay? ... Suddenly, there had to be a reason and I remember someone said that the BBC had banned it in order to not upset George Martin. If, within a couple of years of him writing 'Theme One', some band is coming along with a number one version of his song with a lot of phasing and saxophone and no orchestra – a rock version of it – we thought maybe George wouldn't like that and would say 'Don't play it.' So it seemed to us that the BBC had banned it and probably because George didn't like it. Over the years, it settled as that.

After a long time, though, there was someone who wasn't satisfied with such a theory and decided to follow the question all the way. Phil Smart and Jim Cristopulus, the authors of the English biography of Van der Graaf Generator published in 2005, whilst doing deep research, decided to ask Sir George Martin in person for an explanation. In 1969, Martin had already interrupted his collaboration with EMI to create a new independent structure dedicated to managing audio events, named Air Studios. Previously located in Oxford Street, in the centre of London, the studios then moved in 1992 to the north-western suburb of Hampstead: Martin decided to transform an old Victorian mission school into a big recording studio. Phil and Jim sent a letter to Air Studios, addressed to the Beatles' producer, where they asked if he had ever had the chance to listen to the cover of 'Theme One' made by Van der Graaf Generator and what he thought of it. Surprisingly enough, his answer was pretty prompt and positive:

> I remember that I was absolutely thrilled when I heard that someone had done a cover of 'Theme One'. I was also very intrigued. The original recording had been commissioned for use on the new BBC radio platform, Radio 1, in 1967 and I had written and recorded quite an orchestral-sounding piece. After the launch of Radio One, 'Theme One' was played each day at the start and end of programming and became quite a success, but I never thought anyone would do a cover! Of course, when I heard the Van der Graaf Generator version, I was bowled over. It was a powerful recording that respected the original but – mixed with their own unique style – created a very contemporary piece indeed. All in all, it's a great cover version.

In his conversation with Phil and Jim, he also appeared surprised at the failure of the single, revealing that he had nothing against the broadcasting of it, nor had he been contacted by the BBC regarding the matter. Anyhow, the story that ties Van der Graaf Generator and George Martin has a more personal and certainly funny implication. It happens that one of David

Jackson's children, Jake, started to work at Air Studios in the late 1990s as a sound technician. This had initially caused David some concern. He was worried about any possible resentment by George Martin towards his band and whether it might affect his son's career, as he outlined in the same *Private Conversation* interview:

> By the time Jake left university with all of his engineering qualifications, he gets a job [at Air Studios] and I say to Jake: 'Jake, whatever you do, don't mention Van der Graaf, just in case, because George Martin is the director.' George didn't interview Jake, but he would have known who was joining the staff. 'Don't mention me and don't mention Van der Graaf because if it comes out that you are related to Van der Graaf, he might say 'Get the hell out of here, you're fired!" The son of a Van der Graaf Generator monster...

Years after, though, Jake talked about that with some colleagues, among them George Martin's personal assistant, who had received Phil and Jim's letter. The poor guy asked Jake what to do before handing the letter to his boss, as he was afraid that this could cause him some problems. Luckily, Jake had already become one of the most important sound engineers at Air Studios and was really curious to find out how George would react. David Jackson:

> Jake was so thrilled about George Martin's reaction that, when in 2005, VdGG reunited and there was all the merchandise again, I gave it all to Jake, so he went into the studio wearing a VdGG t-shirt...

Van der Graaf's 'Theme One' obtained good airplay, even on BBC frequencies. In fact, starting in 1978, the most well-known DJ, Tommy Vance, used it as a theme for his popular radio quiz called 'The Friday Night Connection'. In addition, the famous John Peel adopted the Van der Graaf version instead of George Martin's as a closing theme for broadcasts. According to Sean Kelly, the VdGG version of 'Theme One' also began and ended the more grown-up Sounds Of The Seventies broadcasts between 10 pm and 12 pm from Monday through to Friday during the early to late 1970s.

# Live Hearts

> Peter Hammill told me that, although they will include two of the tracks – 'Man Erg' and 'Lemmings' – in their repertoire, they'll only present the other number, 'Saga Of The Lighthouse Keeper', at venues where they can be sure of a totally attentive audience and the right acoustics.
> Roy Carr, *NME*, October 1971

Van der Graaf Generator started playing the *Pawn Hearts* material live well before the album release. Starting from the infamous German tour in May 1971, 'Man-Erg' was added to the setlist and played quite regularly until the sudden break-up in the summer of 1972. The first currently available live recording documenting the song's performance is the one from 10 May at the Circus Krone show in Munich. The 30-minute set comprised only three songs: 'Darkness (11/11)', 'Lost' and 'Man-Erg'. During 'Man-Erg', Hammill played a Hohner Planet N portable electric piano – the 'N' stands for 'natural' as the piano had natural wood finishing. At the time, the Hohner electric piano was quite a common alternative to bringing the much heavier acoustic piano on tour; Tony Banks from Genesis, for instance, used the Planet N as part of his live set in 1972/73 but opted for a 'legless' version that allowed him to place the instrument right on top of the organ.

On 10 June, Van der Graaf Generator included 'Man-Erg' in their Alan Black live studio session for the BBC radio program *Sound Of The Seventies* along with 'Theme One', 'Darkness (11/11)' and one track from the soon-to-be-released first Hammill solo album, *Fool's Mate*, 'Vision'. The session was broadcast on 23 July, almost three months before *Pawn Hearts* was released. After the 1975 reunion, 'Man-Erg' found its way back into the setlist (Hammill now playing a Hohner Clavinet D6 instead of the Planet N). Initially positioned in the first half of the set, during the autumn dates, it was moved to the latter part of the show. Dropped during the 1976 *Still Life* tour and during the first part of the *World Record* tour, this majestic piece of music returned for the October North American tour and was played live during the December 1976 French tour, just before Banton and Jackson left the group. Since the band's reunion in 2005, 'Man-Erg' has been included in every Van der Graaf Generator show as their closing number: the fact that Hammill, Banton and Evans decided to keep it in their live set after David Jackson's departure from the band – despite the prominent role of the saxophone in the song – confirmed how much the three musicians felt most intimately attached to it. I couldn't agree more with my dear friend and huge Van der Graaf Generator fan Mikayel Abazyan, who shared this observation with me:

> During those last ten minutes of the concert, the band, as usual, take us through the corridors of the human being, questioning us: who are we? What is our essence? Angels or killers? Black or white? Having such thoughts in mind and watching the band playing this song, with tears in my eyes, I

> suddenly got the answer to the question I didn't ask. They play this song so often because the band's essence is there. This is their credo. Without this song, they would not be VdGG today. It is their creation through which they praise the Creation and fulfil themselves as true human beings.

Although Van der Graaf Generator did not add it to their setlist until Autumn 1971, 'Lemmings' was going to be another live staple for the band. After the 1975 reunion, the song took a dramatic twist when Hammill started playing the electric guitar on stage instead of the acoustic guitar featured in the original recording, adding a certain roughness to the live arrangement. Every night, the band introduced the track with an impromptu jazz jam that gradually led to the guitar arpeggio that opens the song, much to the surprise and excitement of the audience. 'Lemmings' was regularly played live from the first 2005 reunion show at the London Royal Festival Hall to the 8 May 2022 concert in Padua, Italy.

According to the setlist.fm website, 'Man-Erg' and 'Lemmings' are the two songs that Van der Graaf Generator played live most frequently in their career. Now, when we explore the live outings of *Pawn Hearts*' B-side, we're faced with a different matter…

**March 1972**

It's impossible to know the anticipation that surrounded the live performance of 'A Plague Of Lighthouse Keepers', but surely, after *Pawn Hearts* came out, the band had to confront the inevitability of presenting the complex suite live. According to the band members, Van der Graaf never performed 'Lighthouse Keepers' live in concert at the time. However, later, in 1977, during *The Quiet Zone/The Pleasure Dome* era, the band – featuring Graham Smith on violin and Nic Potter on bass, without Banton or Jackson – actually used to play a medley composed of a few parts of 'A Plague Of Lighthouse Keepers' – 'Eyewitness' and 'The Clot Thickens' – and 'The Sleepwalkers' from the *Godbluff* album.

The only documentation that exists as evidence of a full rendition of the suite in the 1970s dates back to 21 March 1972 when the band recorded a 30-minute studio performance for the Belgian RTB-F TV *Pop Shop* show and were told to play the long suite at a moment's notice. Guy Evans detailed this in *The Book:*

> You always did two TV shows in Belgium because there was a French audience and a Flemish audience. Most European TV shows were pretty jokey – very *Top Of The Pops* – and you were very often miming. It was geared completely towards chart bands, so our expectations weren't very high. We thought they'd want us to play 'Theme One' or 'Refugees' or something. So in the morning, we did the French-speaking show, which was exactly as I described: a mad *Top Of The Pops* thing where we mimed

> something. Then, we went to the Flemish TV show, which was much more of a hippie, underground outfit. And to our astonishment, they were completely set up to film us doing 'A Plague Of Lighthouse Keepers'. So, they filmed us doing 'Theme One' live and then we spent two hours working out 'Lighthouse Keepers' because we hadn't played it in months. We had to re-learn it.

During a 1990 Mick Dillingham interview, David Jackson communicated his memory of the event:

> Whenever we played Europe, there were always offers to do TV shows. There was one time that we turned up at some Belgian TV station and they said to us, 'Ah, you are now ready to do 'Lighthouse Keepers'. We have the candles and sparklers; everything is ready.' We just panicked – nobody had warned us, but there seemed no way out of it, so we did it in sections and edited it together.

Besides the challenge of the execution itself, which the band overcame thanks to their musical mastery, the biggest impediment seemed to be the inevitable technical glitches, as outlined by Hugh Banton in *The Book*:

> It was very difficult; we had to film it in two halves. At that juncture, it was just impossible to set the organ up. We'd done 'Lighthouse Keepers' as a recorded epic with sections strung together, so I found it impossible to play live.

The band's performance was first broadcast on 21 September 1972 and was later aired by Scottish TV in the early 1980s as part of a series called *Rock Of The Seventies*.

If the band's shock when asked to play the song wasn't proof enough of how unusual it was for them to handle side B of *Pawn Hearts* live, further evidence comes from the footage: Hammill himself had to use the lyric sheet originally included with the album, which he placed on the music stand of the electric piano. Oddly enough, there's also a copy of 'The Tin Drum' by Günter Grass on the Hohner Planet music stand. Anyway, the cut Banton refers to was well hidden by the editing, and the band's performance, against all odds, turned out both convincing and entertaining. The sight of Hammill abruptly letting go of his piano playing, raising a glass of red wine and smiling at the camera while the other members wrestle with the grand finale is a sort of manifesto of the unique way the band approached their art. Although formed by four highly skilled musicians, Van der Graaf never aimed for perfection in their live performances, unlike other progressive rock bands such as King Crimson, Genesis or ELP, but were more interested in living the moment and enjoying the act. Anyway, even after countless DVD reissues, the Belgian TV footage is still the most complete document of Van der Graaf Generator at the pinnacle of their deranged creativity.

## March 2013

Exactly 41 years after that performance at the Studios Mathonet in Brussels, a surprise announcement on Peter Hammill's website revealed more details about the band's upcoming European tour:

> VdGG will be performing a couple of long-form pieces at the core of their sets in their upcoming June dates. 'Flight', originally a PH solo/K group piece, has already been aired in North America and Japan last year. It's partly as a result of the reworking of this in the trio format that we've been tempted to go for something even more ambitious ... or dangerous. Our intention is to play 'A Plague Of Lighthouse Keepers', from our 1971 album *Pawn Hearts*, each night. We will not be attempting to recreate the album version but hope to come up with a new, in-the-present approach to this important piece from our past, which has only been played live a handful of times before now. It's a scary prospect but very exciting!'

The reaction to the announcement followed shortly afterwards. In a moment of partial stasis in Van der Graaf's production (*Alt*, released in 2012, included only instrumental improvisations), the idea of pulling 'Lighthouse Keepers' out of their sleeves to elevate their new shows definitely had a galvanising effect on the audience. Among fans, the anticipation for the first show of the tour, scheduled for 16 June in Prague, was enormous. The first clips started to surface during the early hours of the next day, followed by complete footage of the suite in all its glory. The 2013 European tour, soon to be named *The Lighthouse Keepers Tour*, lasted from June to July, reaching six different countries over a total of 14 shows. During the tour, the band played 14 different songs: from that list, 'Flight' (from the 1980 PH solo album *A Black Box*) and 'A Plague Of Lighthouse Keepers' were the only two tracks that were always present in the set. A recording from the tour is available on the official live album *Merlin Atmos*, released on 2 February 2015 by Esoteric Antenna, both on double CD and on single LP.

During the 2013 tour, Van der Graaf arrived in Italy in July for three shows – Udine on 2 July, Milan on 3 July and Pistoia on 5 July. In the course of the last two gigs, I got the opportunity to present my book *Van der Graaf Generator – La Biografia Italiana*, which made an exciting show all the more exciting because of meeting and getting to know so many fans of the band. Some even approached me to share some new details of the infamous 31 May 1972 VdGG concert in Suno (it's remarkable that so many people still remember a show that lasted just a handful of minutes): allegedly, when Evans' drums got hit by a rock thrown on stage, the drummer dived headlong into the audience to fistfight with the culprits ...

How does 'A Plague Of Lighthouse Keepers' fare 42 years later then? The band almost always kept it as a closer – they knew it was the main attraction. Some people were still caught off guard, though, like the legendary photographer Armando Gallo, who sat in front of me at the Live Club in Trezzo in his trademark multicolour shirt and white ponytail. He took pictures, he heartily applauded the band, and when 'Lighthouse Keepers' finally kicked off, he turned around and shouted, 'Oh, oh, oh ... goosebumps!!' The execution was impeccable, if not too schematic at times: there were no significant changes and even the running times of each section matched with the original recording. However, without a doubt, 'Pictures/ Lighthouse', with the ships' dramatic collision and the spectral organ passage that connects it to 'Eyewitness', was alone worth the price of admission. The only notable change came at the very end of the coda: the mind-melting crescendo of 'We Go Now', which dangles suspended, almost unresolved on record, was instead halted abruptly here. The piano arpeggio of 'Eyewitness' then emerged again in a subtly disturbing fashion, leading the way to a baroque closure that felt like a macabre epitaph – Edgar Allan Poe, if he were still alive, would have appreciated it. Those who did not appreciate it in the slightest were the people who came to see the band in Pistoia, let down by a concert that lasted a scarce hour. Contrary to expectations, Van der Graaf had been relegated to opening act for the seemingly endless (more than two hours) performance of Steven Wilson and his band. Rumour has it that there was friction between the trio's entourage and Porcupine Tree's leader, an anomalous situation given that Wilson, in 1992, sampled and used (with permission from Hammill) a portion of 'A Plague Of Lighthouse Keepers' for Porcupine Tree's debut album, *Voyage 34*.

The sense of accomplishment the band felt at the end of their 14-show tour was tangible, as exemplified by Hugh Banton in a 2013 *Private Conversation* interview:

> 'L-K' – as we referred to it this time around! The main challenge was just remembering it all ... however, the strange phenomenon of hand-memory came into play again, whereby you find you can still instinctively remember how to play something that you played regularly in the past, despite decades having gone by. However, of course, we hardly ever played 'L-K' live back in 1971, but clearly, we must have worked hard on it back then in order to be able to play it for that TV show. The main mechanical difficulties in 'L-K' remain as they always have – switching from one section to the next. It's made marginally easier nowadays by being able to press pre-set buttons on the keyboards, or at least it would be if my organ setup wasn't so complicated!

In the same interview, Guy Evans was also positive: 'I thought that Milan was possibly the best one of the tour. Somehow, the choice of songs, the sound

**and the audience involvement all seemed to gell into a special evening.' In a *Private Conversation* interview in January 2014, Peter Hammill spoke of the tour:**

> Well, we all had a degree of trepidation about 'L-K' before doing the tour, especially as we had to announce it (had to, so that we'd be fully committed from the outset) before we'd actually rehearsed it. As always, we still had a number of interesting decisions to make about our approach. As it turned out, I think 'L-K' was marginally less difficult to perform than the companion piece, 'Flight'. And we'd well mastered that by this tour, of course! ... It's the usual thing: the music starts, you dive right in and you emerge, somehow, out at the other end. Normal feelings don't really come into it. Especially with VdGG, there's never actually time to think or analyse in the middle of the act!!

## Discography/Pawn Hearts

As an appendix to this essay, I have provided a discography focused on the *Pawn Hearts* album and on the 'Theme One'/'W' 7" single. Back in the 1970s, Van der Graaf Generator's albums were pressed in a wide amount of different countries, and as a consequence, different editions were often released. Switching to the digital format, the first CD editions were published between 1987 and 1989 by Virgin, followed in 2005 by the remastered versions by Virgin/EMI that also included some interesting bonus tracks. A newly remastered version of *Pawn Hearts*, as well as a completely remixed one by Stephen W Tayler – both in Stereo and in 5.1 Surround Sound – were released in 2021 as part of the *Van der Graaf Generator – The Charisma Years 1970-1978* boxset.

**Pawn Hearts** (1971, 12")
**Side One**
'Lemmings (Including Cog)' (Hammill)
'Man-Erg' (Hammill)

**Side Two**
'A Plague Of Lighthouse Keepers'
a) 'Eyewitness' (Hammill)
b) 'Pictures/Lighthouse' (Jackson/Banton)
c) 'Eyewitness' (Hammill)
d) 'S.H.M.' (Hammill)
e) 'Presence Of The Night' (Hammill)
f) 'Kosmos Tours' (Evans)
g) '(Custard's) Last Stand' (Hammill)
h) 'The Clot Thickens' (Hammill/Band)
i) 'Land's End (Sineline)' (Jackson)
l) 'We Go Now' (Jackson/Banton)

All arrangements by the band

Hugh Banton: Hammond E & C, Farfisa Professional organs, piano, Mellotron, ARP synthesiser, bass pedals, bass guitar, psychedelic razor, vocals
Guy Evans: drums, timpani, percussion, piano
Peter Hammill: lead vocals, acoustic and slide guitar, electric piano, piano
David Jackson: tenor, alto and soprano saxophones and devices, flute, vocals

With Robert Fripp: electric guitar
Producer: John Anthony
Engineers: Robin Cable, David Hentschel, Ken Scott
Tape Op: Mike and Dave C.
Brightest Hope: Howard

Cover: Paul Whitehead/Cleen Mashine Studios
Photography: Keith Morris!
Recorded at Trident Studios, London W. 1. July through September 1971, aided and abetted by Nohjndijcrackycracky*
B&C Records Ltd, 37 Soho Square, London W1
Sleeve printed and made by the E.J. Day Group, London and Bedford

*'Nohjndijcrackycracky was an appalling misprint for Nohjnohjcrackycracky, a catchphrase for our then roadies, Nohj and Cracky, two sons of the Leek who have since left us ... no real mystery!!!' (www.vandergraafgenerator.co.uk)

## First Pressing

Charisma – CAS 1051 – 1971

The album was originally released in the UK in October 1971 on Charisma CAS 1051, pink scroll label. The gatefold cover includes the infamous infra-red shot that the band and Keith Morris did at Crowborough. Sadly, Morris went missing from a dive on a submarine wreck in the English Channel around 17 June 2005. The album credits are positioned in the left, bottom corner of the picture, framed by a thin white line. The lyrics were printed on a 12 x 12 square black sheet of paper, the same size as the album cover, which was included only in the first press run. The lyric sheet was also made available by post to people who sent a stamped addressed envelope. It was possible to find out about the offer from the main UK music papers, such as *Melody Maker*.

## Further And Local Pressings

### UK

Charisma (1971) – CAS 1051
Virgin (1987) – CHC 54

The second UK pressing is still a gatefold one, but the label features the well-known Mad Hatter image (taken from the original figures that Sir John Tenniel painted for the Lewis Carroll book *Alice In Wonderland*) instead of the pink scroll one. From the third pressing onward, Phonogram is featured on the label, as B&C were no longer taking care of the distribution. In 1987, in conjunction with the first pressing of the whole Van der Graaf Generator catalogue on CD, Virgin decided to also release a new vinyl pressing using the CHC ('Charisma Classics') code. The artwork remains the same as the older versions, except for the label, which features a new Charisma logo and the Mad Hatter picture in a smaller size.

### Italy

Philips (1972) – 6369 915 L
Charisma (1972) – 6369 915 L

The album was released in Italy in January 1972 (on the vinyl run-out groove, the master is credited as being created on 7 January 1972) on the usual

Philips blue label. The sleeve is not gatefold, so the credits are printed in red on the back cover. A plain 'Pawn Hearts. Van der Graaf Generator' is titled along the top. A couple of months later, the album was printed in Italy straight on the Charisma Mad Hatter label, keeping the same catalogue number and artwork. On both versions, the only way to learn the song titles is to read them on the labels.

**Germany**

Philips (1972) – 6369 915
Virgin (1984) – 207 110-270

The German edition of the album was released on Philips blue label and in gatefold format. What's peculiar about this edition is that both the credits and the lyrics were printed in white on the inside picture of the band (left side). The 1984 Virgin reissue lacked the gatefold format and the lyrics, while the song titles and credits were featured on the back cover.

**Holland**

Charisma (1972) – 6321 125

Though the Holland edition was also on Charisma, the catalogue number is different. The label featured the Mad Hatter image and the packaging was the single sleeve version.

**US**

Charisma (1972) – CAS 1051

As we already pointed out, the main feature of the US edition was that 'Theme One' was harshly placed between 'Lemmings' and 'Man-Erg' on side A, much to Hammill's annoyance. The first pressing was on the Charisma Pink Scroll label and in gatefold format; the second pressing was on the Mad Hatter label, also as a gatefold. The third pressing was the single-sleeve version.

**Canada**

Buddah Records (1972) – CAS 1051
GRT/Charisma (1972) – 9211-1051

As for the US edition, the Canadian one also featured 'Theme One' on side A between 'Lemmings' and 'Man-Erg' and came in the usual gatefold format. However, the image on the label was different: a Buddha on a pink background. Furthermore, the record was actually tucked into a pocket inside the gatefold cover rather than on the outside, so the only way to access it was to open the sleeve wide and extract the vinyl from left to right.

**Brazil**

Charisma (1972) – 6369 915

The artwork for this edition was completely different from the others. In fact, the front cover featured the whole Paul Whitehead painting on a black background. The name of the band and the album title were written using the same font as the first pressing, placed above and below the image. The back sleeve featured a part of the Crowborough band shot originally included in the gatefold edition (this edition is a single sleeve). The label is the Mad Hatter one.

**Spain**

Philips (1972) – 63 69 915 promo
Charisma (1978) – 63 69 915
The album was released in Spain in 1972 by Philips, but in a promo version only, featuring different artwork. The band picture by Keith Morris was on the front cover, framed by a white background that also included the album title and the name of the band. The back sleeve was all in white and featured the tracklist. The label was the Philips blue one. At a later stage (1978), the album was officially released by Charisma in the usual gatefold sleeve and Mad Hatter label.

**Australia**

Philips (1972) – 6369 915
The gatefold sleeve edition on the Philips blue label.

**Greece**

Charisma (1971) – 6369 915
The single-sleeve edition on the Charisma Mad Hatter label.

**New Zealand**

Philips (1972) – 6369 915
The single-sleeve edition on the Philips blue label. Distributed by Polygram.

The *Pawn Hearts* album was also reissued on double 180-gram vinyl by Plastic Head (2012 – PCV 006 LP) on the Cargo Records and Back on Black labels, apparently in a limited run of 1000 copies. 4 Men With Beards (2012 – 4M 218) took care of the vinyl reissue in the US, this time on single vinyl. Both editions feature the original artwork and include the remastered audio from the 2005 Virgin/EMI CD reissue. The double vinyl reissue includes the CD bonus tracks.

**Other Formats**

**Cassette**

Philips (1972) – 7164 006
Charisma (1984) – CASMC 106 double play with *Still Life*
Virgin (1987) – CHCK 7054
The distinctive trait of the *Pawn Hearts* cassette edition is that the two vinyl sides are presented in reverse order: 'A Plague Of Lighthouse Keepers' is on

the A side and the two other tracks are on the B side. In 1984, Charisma released the album as a 'double play' with *Still Life* on a single tape, while the final cassette version was printed in 1987 as a companion release to the 'Charisma Classic' vinyl edition.

**Stereo 8**
Charisma (1971) – Y8CAS 1051

**Compact Disc**
Virgin/Charisma (1987) – CASCD 1051, 0777 787549 2 3
Virgin/EMI/Charisma (2005) – CASCDR 1051, 7243 4 74890 2 0
Virgin/EMI/Charisma (2005) – VJCP-68759 mini-LP replica
The first digital reissue did not include bonus tracks, whereas the 2005 remaster featured as many as five bonus tracks:

'Theme 1' (Original Version)
'W' (Alternative Take)
'Angle Of Incidents' (Unreleased)
'Ponker's Theme' (Unreleased)
'Diminutions' (Unreleased)

The 2005 Japanese CD version (VJCP) was edited in the usual mini-LP replica.

The 2021 *Van der Graaf Generator – The Charisma Years 1970-1978* boxset featured a newly remastered version of *Pawn Hearts*, as well as a completely remixed one by Stephen W Tayler – both in Stereo and in 5.1 Surround Sound.

The album was released also in the SHM (Super High Material CD) and SACD format. The DSD flat transfer from the UK original analogue master tapes was used.

**'Theme One'** (1972, 7")
Side One
1. 'Theme One' (Martin)
2. 'W' (Hammill)

**First Pressing**
Charisma – CB 175 – 1972
The 'Theme One' 7" was released in the UK on 4 February 1972 on the classic Charisma pink scroll label. The cover image is the same as the one included in the gatefold version of *Pawn Hearts* but cropped and printed in red on a blue background. The back cover features the name of the band, the record title and images of the Van der Graaf Generator albums already published by

Charisma (*The Least We Can Do Is Wave To Each Other*, *H To He Who Am The Only One* and *Pawn Hearts*) and Peter Hammill's *Fool's Mate* cover.

## Local Pressings

### Italy

Philips (1972) – 6073 311

The 'Theme One' 7" was released in Italy on 15 February 1972, just after the first Van der Graaf Generator Italian tour. The front cover features a new and surreal image: a disoriented man's face with pawns flowing from his open mouth. The writing on the top left is also worth noticing: 'If you happen to meet a mountain of applause, that's only for the wonderful Van der Graaf Generator'. The back cover showcases an advert for *Pawn Hearts* and the album cover. The label is the usual Philips blue one. 'Theme One' was released in Italy as a Juke Box version (Philips AS 140), with Leon Russell's 'A Hard Rain's Gonna Fall' as a B-Side. The Italian music journalist Ernesto Assante had a vivid memory of that:

> It was the summer of 1972. I was still a child and I was spending my holidays in Procida, as usual. At the bar near the restaurant, there was a jukebox: 50 lire to play one song, 100 lire to play three songs. To my surprise, among the songs available to play, there was 'Theme One' by Van der Graaf Generator. I was kind of addicted to jukebox playing, so that summer, I spent a lot of coins and most of them were on Van der Graaf.

'Theme One' was also played as a jingle during the famous Italian radio show *Per Voi Giovani*, when Carlo Massarini and Raffaele Cascone were leading the program. It was the soundtrack to the slogan by Cascone: 'Per Voi Giovani, Il Rock Del Mediterraneo!' (For the young: Mediterranean Rock!)

### France

Philips Série Parade (1972) – 6073 311

This was the mono version, which is much sought after by fans and collectors. The cover featured a picture of an outdoor shot of the band in a round frame on a blue background. The name of the band in red was curved around the top of the frame, while the titles of the tracks were written in white. On the completely white back cover, there was a small bit of writing – 'A Charisma recording' – and some logos. The label was Philips Série Parade, the blue background being lighter compared to the Italian one.

### Germany

Philips (1972) 6073 311

Another different cover – a beautiful, full-colour one of the four members of the band in the countryside – adorned this version of the single. Everyone in the image is wearing a hat. The name of the band and the titles of the tracks were written in a powerful blue and red font, backed by yellow sparks. The back cover was devoted to advertising. The label was the classic Philips blue one, but the blue background was lighter compared to the Italian one and similar to the French edition.

### Australia

Philips (1972) – 6073 311
This was also the mono version. The vinyl was housed in a generic CBS sleeve. The label was the Philips blue one.

### Digital Reissues

'Theme One' was available in a digital format for the first time in 1986 as part of the Virgin compilation *Van der Graaf Generator Scenes From 1969/71* (COMCD 2), which introduced the digital reissue of the whole VdGG catalogue. The B-Side, 'W', was instead released in a digital format in 1993 on the *I Prophesy Disaster* (CDVM 9026) Van der Graaf compilation. Both tracks were also included in the VdGG box set *The Box* (2000), though 'Theme One' is from a 1971 BBC Session live recording. An alternate take of 'W' and a slightly different mix of 'Theme One' (without the pipe organ and synthesiser tracks) were featured as bonus tracks on the 2005 remastered version of *Pawn Hearts* and on the 2021 *Charisma Years* box set.

The original George Martin version of 'Theme One' is available in digital format on the compilation *The Sound Gallery Vol.2* (1996), distributed by EMI, and as part of the boxset *Produced By George Martin – 50 Years In Recording*.

## Bibliography


### Books

Carnelli, P., *Van der Graaf Generator – Behind & Beyond: Le Storie Dietro Le Copertine* (Iacobelli, 2022).
Carnelli, P., *Van der Graaf Generator – La Biografia Italiana* (Arcana, 2013)
Christopulos, J. and Smart, P., *The Book* (Phil And Jim Publishing, 2005).
Coffey, D., *Van der Graaf Generator On Track* (Sonicbond, 2020).
Fiaccavento, L. and Olivotto, M., *Dark Figures Running – Tutti I Testi 1968/1978* (Ph/VdGG Study Group, 2005).
Fiaccavento, L. and Maestri, E., *Fogwalking – Tutti I Testi 1971/1980* (Ph/VdGG Study Group, 2013).
Hammill, P., *Killers Angels Refugees* (Charisma Books, 1974).
Odriozola, R., *A Musical Guide To Pawn Hearts By Van der Graaf Generator* (Spaceward Records 2007).

### Magazines

**Melody Maker**

27 March 1971 – 'Six Bob gigs which made Van der Graaf' by Richard Williams
April 1971 – 'Caught in the act: Van der Graaf' by Chris Welch
6 November 1971 – 'A Plague of Lighthouse Keepers' by Roy Hollingworth
August 1972 – 'Van breaks down by Richard Williams'
7 April 1973 – 'Keep an eye on Hammill' by Roy Hollingworth

**NME**

February 1971 – 'Surprise package' by Roy Carr
October 1971 – 'Generator hotter' by Roy Carr

**O.D. Magazine**

Issue 1, summer 1976 – 'A million miles away and yesterday' by Jonathan Barnett

**Pilgrims**

Issue 9, November 1990 – 'Pawn Hearts part 1' by Dean Carter
Issue 10, February 1991 – 'Pawn Hearts part 2' by Dean Carter
Issue 12, July 1991 – 'Pawn Hearts yet another reprise'
1997 – 'Paul Whitehead interview' by Jim Christopulos

**Ptolemaic Terrascope**

Issue 2, May 1991 – 'Van der Graaf Generator: the David Jackson interview' by Mick Dillingham

**Record Mirror**

May 1971 – 'The Generator are staying very content on the continent' by Keith Altham

December 1971 – 'Van der Graaf Generator, Pawn Hearts' by B.M.

**Sounds**
29 January 1972 – 'Van der Graaf opening a chink in the curtain' by Steve Peacock

**Suono**
Issue 477, June 2013 – 'Il ritorno del guardiano del faro' by Paolo Carnelli

**Wonderous Stories**
Issue 16, December 2009 – 'Theme One e altre storie' by Paolo Carnelli

**Would you like to write for Sonicbond Publishing?**

We are mainly a music publisher, but we also occasionally publish in other genres including film and television. At Sonicbond Publishing we are always on the look-out for authors, particularly for our two main series, On Track and Decades.

Mixing fact with in depth analysis, the On Track series examines the entire recorded work of a particular musical artist or group. All genres are considered from easy listening and jazz to 60s soul to 90s pop, via rock and metal.

The Decades series singles out a particular decade in an artist or group's history and focuses on that decade in more detail than may be allowed in the On Track series.

While professional writing experience would, of course, be an advantage, the most important qualification is to have real enthusiasm and knowledge of your subject. First-time authors are welcomed, but the ability to write well in English is essential.

Sonicbond Publishing has distribution throughout Europe and North America, and all our books are also published in E-book form. Authors will be paid a royalty based on sales of their book. Further details about our books are available from www.sonicbondpublishing.com. To contact us, complete the contact form there or email info@sonicbondpublishing.co.uk